H. von Holst

The French Revolution Tested by Mirabeau's Career

Twelve lectures on the history of the French revolution, delivered at the Lowell institute,

Boston, Mass.

H. von Holst

The French Revolution Tested by Mirabeau's Career
Twelve lectures on the history of the French revolution, delivered at the Lowell institute, Boston, Mass.

ISBN/EAN: 9783743407169

Manufactured in Europe, USA, Canada, Australia, Japa

Cover: Foto ©ninafisch / pixelio.de

Manufactured and distributed by brebook publishing software (www.brebook.com)

H. von Holst

The French Revolution Tested by Mirabeau's Career

Dedicated

TO

MY WIFE,

ANNIE ISABELLE, *née* HATT,

IN TOKEN OF GRATITUDE

FOR THE SYMPATHY AND AID

GIVEN ME FOR TWENTY-TWO YEARS

IN MY LITERARY LABORS.

PREFATORY NOTE.

READERS and critics are respectfully requested to take these pages for what they purport to be: not a book on the history of the French Revolution, but merely some lectures on it, composed principally with a view to illustrating and criticising some of its main features by the opinions and the career of the foremost political genius of its first phase. By the terms of Mr. Augustus Lowell's invitation, I was confined to twelve lectures and for each lecture to one hour. The work had to be done with these limitations constantly in mind. Fair critics will remember this, judging me by what I have accomplished within the compass allowed me, and not as the author of a book with as many pages at his disposal as he chooses to fill. I have added some notes, partly referring the reader to some of my authorities—principally the original sources—and partly furnishing some illustrations of and vouchers for the statements in the text. The body of the lectures I have left wholly unchanged, because I publish them in compliance with the wishes of many of those who heard them delivered, and they desired me to publish what they had heard me say, and not what I might have said. This accounts for some peculiarities of style. I have amply availed myself of the liberties deemed admissible in speaking. But I have undoubtedly taken also other liberties with the English language, simply because I did not know any better. Will the reader kindly grant my request to judge these leniently? I have deemed it justifiable to lay the greater stress upon having the What exactly as I wanted it to be, rather than to have other people file the How into such smooth and idiomatic English that an easy critic might have mistaken me for a native American. I was afraid of their filing away rather more of my What than I cared to let go.

H. VON HOLST.

TABLE OF CONTENTS.
Vol. I.

LECTURE	PAGE
I. The Heritage of Louis XIV and Louis XV	1
II. Paris and Versailles	45
III. Mending the Old Garment with New Cloth	82
IV. The Revolution *before* the Revolution	128
V. A Typical Family Tragedy of Portentous Historical Import	164
VI. The States-General; a Rudderless Craft in a Storm-tossed Sea	219

THE FRENCH REVOLUTION.

TESTED BY

THE CAREER OF MIRABEAU.

LECTURE I.

The Heritage of Louis XIV. and Louis XV.

"The Lord is . . . visiting the iniquity of the fathers upon the children unto the third and fourth generation."[1]

WHO cannot recall some hour in his life, when he has felt tempted to revolt against this awful announcement as an incomprehensible law emanating from a just God—doubly incomprehensible, because His name is also Love and Mercy? It requires, however, but a moment's reflection to see that, though it is surely awe-inspiring, there is so

[1] Numbers xiv. 18.

little incomprehensible about it that it would be more justifiable to call it the statement of a self-evident truth. What is it, but another formulation of the one law pervading and dominating everything that exists, the law of evolution, which is itself, in a sense, only another form of saying that causes have effects, and that the character of the effects is determined by the nature of the causes? History is one continuous proof of the truth of this proposition, and from some chapters of it, it glares forth with overwhelming force. The very first place among these is unquestionably held by that of the French Revolution. On every page of it is stamped in letters of fire the warning: Beware; for what you sow, your children must reap.

It was a fearful heritage that Louis XIV. and Louis XV. left to Louis XVI., and a person more unfit to administer it could hardly be conceived of. It was of such a character, that of necessity his very virtues had to work as a curse to himself and to his country.

If we are to judge by what is revealed to the first glance, a simpler political structure than that of France under the *ancien régime* is not conceivable. It was the logical realization of Louis

XIV's maxim: "*L'Etat c'est moi,*"[1]—I am the state. Louis XV. fully maintained this claim. He asserted: "In my person alone resides the sovereign authority... To me alone belongs the legislative power without dependence and without division.[2] The constitution of the commonwealth in its entirety[3] emanates from me."[4] So far as this really ever had been the law of the realm, it was still so, when Louis XVI. ascended the throne. His two predecessors had reigned in such a manner as if it were the unchallenged and incontestable law of the land, and far into the reign of Louis XV. the people had in the main virtually acquiesced in this claim of the crown. This was

[1] According to the interesting and instructive work, *L'Esprit dans l'Histoire*, by Ed. Fournier, the authorship of the phrase is wrongly attributed to Louis XIV. The assertion is probably correct. Historians, however, will, in spite of that, certainly never cease calling it his maxim, and justly so, for though he may not have used just these words, they graphically and succinctly express the idea which unquestionably was the underlying principle of his whole political feeling, thought, and action.

[2] "Sans partage," *i.e.*, without any one else having a share in it.

[3] My knowledge of English is not sufficient to find a better rendering of "*l'ordre public tout entier*." "The whole public order" seems to me ambiguous, if it be at all idiomatic.

[4] *Lit. de justice* of 3d March, 1766. Taine: Les Origines de la France contemporaine, I., p. 16.

in itself enough to render it more and more a curse, for, with the progress of civilization, the identification of the person of the sovereign with the state, must, in every relation of life, necessarily become more and more a palpable lie. The law, however, is the basis of the state. So far as the law and the facts become discordant, the foundation under the edifice is broken down. And here the law itself was a lie. Unrestricted absolutism was only the actual condition of France. Under the all-enveloping cover of royal absolutism lay a chaotic tangle of recognized rights—recognized not as a free act of grace, but as a legal fact transmitted with the crown from king to king.

The French people were legally a nation only in so far as they had one sovereign. "We want at least to be a nation," said Mirabeau on the 21st of January, 1789, in the provincial estates of the Provence.[1] France had a fourfold division; the ecclesiastical—the oldest, partly dating back to

---

[1] Méjan: Collection complète des travaux de M. Mirabeau l'ainé à l'Assemblée nationale, I. 3. For brevity's sake I shall hereafter quote this collection as *Œuvres*.—Calonne, in his speech on the opening of the Assembly of Notables (Febr. 22, 1787), said: "Quand on considère par quels accroissements successifs, par quelle réunion de contrées diversement gouvernées, le royaume est parvenu à sa consistance actuelle, on ne doit pas être étonné de la diversité des ré-

the times of the Carolingians; that in provinces —being the historical geography and therefore the deepest rooted in the heads and hearts of the people by traditions, customs, sentiments, and, to no inconsiderable extent, even in institutions and laws; the judicial; and, finally, the administrative, principally upon a financial basis. There being no organic relation between the four divisions, their boundary lines frequently crossed each other in the wildest manner and without any underlying general principle, those of the frontier dioceses not even coinciding with those of the state. And not only geographically, but also in regard to their functions and powers they were matted into a bewildering maze. The ecclesiastical authority did not originate with the state. The church was a state within the state, claiming even higher authority, and yet not only connected with it in a manner establishing an organic interdependence between them, but also actually and legally subject to it. Turning to the provinces the first thing we notice is that they present constitutionally two groups, those with provincial estates, the so-called *pays d'état*, and those without such

gimes, de la multitudes des formes hétérogènes, et de l'incohérence des principes, qui en désunissent les parties."

estates, the *pays d'élection*. Within each category the differences were innumerable. As constituent parts of the state their legal position greatly differed. From one point of view France was in the highest degree a consolidated state, and yet there was in all provinces something or other that was more or less incompatible with the thoroughly organic character implied in the idea of a consolidated state. The Provence had even musty documents establishing beyond contradiction her right to pass herself off as a distinct "nation," and she still attempted to insist upon its recognition, when the revolutionary tempest commenced to sweep over the land. Even in regard to taxation France was an incongruous jumble, and in some most essential respects internal duties put the different parts of the kingdom into the relation of foreign states towards each other.—To speak of a judicial *system* in the *ancien régime* is about as unsuitable as to say the effulgence of darkness. The competency of the courts not clearly defined, conflicts of jurisdiction too common to be characterized as exceptions, the law very far from being the same throughout the country, but everywhere Roman, statutory, and customary law mixed up in a forbidding mess. To speak of a common law would, of course, be utterly inappropriate; for it is said that the different systems of customary law in force reached the appalling figure of something over four hundred.[1] And above all law the sovereign pleasure of the king interfering with the regular administration of justice by instituting special courts for the adjudication of special cases, whenever he deemed fit, and he strongly inclined to see fit when high state officials were parties to the case.[2]

The courts could not prevent the scales and the sword being wrenched out of their hands by this and other means, but they could protest, and that they frequently did most energetically. Besides protesting, they could, however, also give tit for tat, and they did not fail to do that either. They were not confined to the administering of justice,

[1] Other estimates are even much higher. Cassagnac: Histoire des Causes de la Révolution, states that 530 are mentioned in the *Coutumier général,* and he thinks this figure too low.

[2] I have seen in the National Archives in the Temple many reports from intendants strongly urging upon the government to make it an invariable rule, that no state officials were to be dragged before the ordinary courts, because that greatly tended to diminish the people's respect for the government.—Also, persons of rank, who were not officials, were frequently shielded from justice either by quashing the proceedings, or by referring the cause to the king.

but had also administrative and even legislative power. How far these extended had, however, never been authoritatively settled. Hence constant encroachments and eternal conflicts. These often came to a dangerous point through the concurrent legislative power exercised by the highest courts, called Parliaments, and more especially by that of Paris, in the form of registering the royal edicts. This legislative power was utterly devoid of any positive character. Even to say that it gave the Parliaments a negative upon the legislative will of the king, a veto power, would grossly overshoot the mark. It was only a legal means of passive resistance. And even as such it did not rest upon a positive legal basis. The right was purely a historical growth, so firmly established, that its existence was not contested by the crown; but neither its constitutional nature nor its extent had ever been determined. The inevitable consequence was incessant wrangling without the possibility of ever coming to a legal settlement of the controversy. While the crown did not deny that to impart in the regular way legal force to its edicts, their registration by the Parliament was required,[1] the Parliament did not

[1] The exact time when the practice originated is not

deny that it was in duty bound to register whenever the king in person ordered it to do so in a so-called *lit de justice*, bed of justice. But in such a case the registering by no means always ended the strife even as to the question directly at issue. Fresh remonstrances were often sent up to the throne, sharply denouncing the abuse of power, and eventually, in strange inconsistency, even branding it as illegal, though not calling into question the right to impose obedience in a " bed of justice." The government, on the other hand, was apt to get exasperated and to cut the knot by sending the Parliament into exile. Sooner or later, the quarrel was then terminated for the time being by some compromise or other, only to recommence with increased acrimony at the first opportunity that offered itself.

The result of all this was constant unrest and excitement, ever growing, though for a long time unconscious longing for real nationalization, and

---

known, because in 1618 the oldest registers were destroyed in a fire which consumed the Hôtel de Ville. Originally the edicts were deposited in the *chartrier*. The vicissitudes frequently experienced by this in times of war demonstrated the necessity of providing in some other way for the preservation of the authentic text. Merely for this purpose they were *enregistré* with the *greffe* of the Parliament.

a steady progress in the sapping of the sense of right (*Rechtsbewusztsein*). Surely, the facts amply justified Mirabeau's solemn warning in the National Assembly, to keep well in mind how "formidable the monstrous alliance between judicial and political powers" has been "to our fathers and to ourselves."[1]

There is, however, still another side to the picture. If we look closer, it at once becomes apparent that there was much more ado than real activity in the jostling throng of authorities, and that the excessive diversity of conditions was in the main only a deceptive semblance.

To Tocqueville belongs the merit of having first discovered and proved that the immoderate centralization, which up to our times has been so eminently characteristic of France, was not the work of the revolution, but existed already under the *ancien régime*. The essential difference between the two periods in this respect consists in this, that the revolution made legal what under the *ancien régime* was to a great extent only a fact.

All the threads of the governmental apparatus issued from and terminated in the council of the king (*conseil du roi*). The council's authority,

[1] Œuvres, I., 452, July 24, 1789.

however, did not rest upon any legal basis. Legally it had only to execute the king's orders. In him alone resided all power. "*Car tel est mon plaisir*"—for such is my pleasure—this official formula of the governmental decrees was not an empty figure of speech; it was in full, in terrible accord with the facts. In the council the *contrôleur général*, though not prime minister, was in a measure the centre around which everything turned. His power was greater and more comprehensive than that of a modern minister of the finances. He exercised a controlling influence upon nearly everything that stood in any relation to the finances, and almost everything pertaining to administration is in some way or other connected with them. He might be properly called *the* administrator of the kingdom; and under the *ancien régime* the administering was extended practically to everything.

What the *contrôleur général* was for the whole state, the intendant was for its administrative subdivision, the *généralité*. He had his hand in everything, and always in the spirit of bustling, distrustful, and presumptuous paternalism. There was nothing the intendant did not do or control. He allotted the taxes; he directed the levying of the militia, determining not only the percentage each community had to furnish of the whole quota of the *généralité*, but also who was to shoulder the musket and who could go home; he by means of the *maréchaussée* took care of the maintenance of public order; he directed all the public works; he distributed what the government appropriated for the support of the poor; he opened or shut the doors of the public workhouses to the indigent; he told the peasant how the government wanted him to till his field and feed his cattle; he ordered bonfires to be lit, and fined those who had not gone to the *Te Deum;* he advised the municipalities, which officially still enjoyed self-government, whom to elect to the municipal offices, and they never dared to have a will of their own; he alone could give permission to call a communal meeting; through him the community had to ask the permission of the council to spend money for any municipal purpose, even if it were but 25*l.*, and often years passed by ere it was allowed to repair the rotten roof of the parsonage or the tottering steeple of the parish church

Surely, this governmental machinery was simple enough,—ay, it was of a fearful, paralyzing, nay absolutely killing simplicity. Turgot, speaking of villages, said: "A community is a mass of hovels and inhabitants of them, these not less passive than those." And this listless passivity pervaded the whole body politic in all its parts. *The capability for self-government was systematically annihilated.* And it was done so successfully that the people at last could not get enough of this kind of paternalism. We meet with bitter complaints that, in regard to one thing or another, the government had not marked out the way with sufficient clearness and strictness. On the other hand, however, the kicking against the pricks never ceased, because, while the essence of self-government was destroyed, its forms were partly left standing.[1] The incompatibility of the two statements is only apparent. The human mind being what it is, nothing is more common than such self-contradictions. The acting and reacting of the two conflicting tendencies upon each other resulted in the belief that anything can be accomplished by legislation, and in gauging the government by this standard. As the government charged itself with

---

[1] In my opinion Mr. Edw. L. Lowell, in his excellent book, The Eve of the French Revolution, lays too much stress upon these forms, and does not fully realize to what a degree they had become empty shells.

attending to everything, it was of course also held responsible for everything. Commanding, instructing, or at least advising in regard to everything, was it not also its duty to foresee everything up to the fancies of fashion, the whims of trade, the freaks of the weather? The government became the terrestrial Providence.

One of the attributes of Providence is omnipresence. If we merely look at the intendants and their subordinates, who did nearly all the real governing, we get but a very inadequate idea of how far government under the *ancien régime* came up to this requirement. I say government, and not *the* government, intending thereby to indicate that I now want the word to be understood in its most comprehensive sense. There was such an innumerable host of all sorts of public officials, that one is tempted to say, whatever a man did, he was almost as sure to have some kind of a public functionary at his side, as he was to be followed by his own shadow. If the peasant brought an ox to market, the inspector of cattle presented himself; the inspector of calves looked after the calves; the inspector of swine took care of the pigs, and if it happened to be a sow with young he was joined by the inspector of sucking pigs. And thus all over. These men were public officers, not for the purpose of serving any public interest; that was at best quite a secondary consideration. For show and as a legal title to lucre, the mantle of authority was thrown around their shoulders. The mad practice of selling public offices—largely extended even to the army—had generated this ulcer, which gradually, but steadily, worked its way from the surface to the very bones, more and more infecting and vitiating the whole blood of the body politic. The demand for this kind of goods being always in excess of the supply, the handiest means for procuring money in an emergency was to sell offices. Unfortunately, the emergencies grew more frequent and more pressing. The consequence was, that the government commenced to create offices merely for the purpose of selling them. This was even worse than selling captaincies and judgeships. The army and the bench and the bar had real work to do, and were, in a sense, close corporations, pervaded by a strong sense of corporative honor, upheld by the mighty incentive to hand down untarnished to posterity the glorious record of the past. The latter were even to no inconsiderable extent provided with the legal means of protecting themselves against the pollution of having unworthy elements engrafted upon them merely for the sake of getting their money.[1] Those other offices, however, were of a purely parasitical nature. They were wholly devoid of any moral element. Having no reason to exist, they were immoral *ab initio*. That the government was well aware of this is proved by the fact that, when circumstances permitted, it proceeded to suppress them by paying back the purchase money, frequently, however, also doing more or less violence to vested rights.[2] This was even by no means confined to offices of this kind. Public corporations were treated no better than individuals. Even the franchises of cities were sold, suppressed, and resold—all for the purpose of getting money. The trouble was that financial distress became in such measure the rule, and attained so high a degree, that the ingenuity of the government was taxed to the utmost in inventing new offices.[3]

---

[1] In a measure the monopoly of the nobility as to commissions worked in the same direction in regard to the army.

[2] Richelieu is said to have suppressed 100,000.

[3] When the minister Desmarest proposed to Louis XIV. the creation of some new offices, the king was so struck by

It would require a vivid imagination to overestimate the evil consequences of the vicious practice thus developed into methodical madness by the fostering influences of untoward circumstances.[1] As to the offices that entailed real, necessary, and highly-important work, the government had for a mess of pottage, partially relinquished the right of direct control over its organs. Though this was certainly of great import, the other results were even more baleful. The government ate up to-day what of right belonged to the morrow. The social distinction conferred by the office went for something, and indeed for a good deal, in making it salable and getting a satisfactory price for it. The *ancien régime* had

the utter lack of any *raison d'être* in them that he asked: "Qui est-ce qui achetera ces charges?" The minister replied: "Votre majesté ignore une des plus belles prérogatives des rois de France, qui est que, lorsqu'un roi crée une charge, Dieu crée à l'instant un sot pour l'acheter."—Archives Parlementaires, I. 125.

[1] It is worthy of notice that Montesquieu nevertheless defended it. His reason for doing so is very suggestive. "Or, dans une monarchie où, quand les charges ne se vendraient pas par un réglement public, l'indigence ou l'avidité des courtisans les vendraient tout de même, le hasard donnera de meilleurs sujets que le choix du prince; enfin la manière de s'avancer par les richesses inspire et entretien l'industrie, chose dont cette espèce de gouvernement a grand besoin."—Archives Parlem., I. 125.

with eminent success nursed the national susceptibility for outward honors into morbid vanity. As a rule, however, the purchasers also required something more substantial for their money. One way of remunerating them was to allow them fees, *i. e.*, the people were made to pay them directly the interest of the capital invested in the office. By another they were made to do it indirectly. Tax-privileges of some kind or other, frequently also nobility,[1] which was a synonym for exemption from certain pecuniary and other onerous and well-hated obligations towards the state, were acquired with the office. Now the embarrassments of the treasury being the cause of making offices a merchandise, it goes without saying that the government could not afford to lose what it could no longer levy from its office-customers. The rest of the people had to make up what they failed to pay: the strong were relieved of their just share in the public burdens by strapping it to the shoulders of the weak in addition to their own fair portion. The evil economical consequences were not to be made light of, but in comparison to the moral effects

---

[1] According to Necker, 4,070 offices conferred nobility.—De l'Administration des Finances, III. 145.

they were of only small account. Owing to all the attendant circumstances alluded to, the outcome of the selling of offices may be summed up thus : ever growing obscuration of the proper conception of self-government, accompanied by an ever diminishing longing for it ; ever progressing decay of the sense of right ; constant tightening of the tax-screw upon the masses ; steady extension and aggravation of the bane of privilege, and ever deepening irritation of the people at the smarts and ravages inflicted upon it by this scourge ; ever widening alienation of the people from a government and a political system imposing upon it all these plagues.

The flood-gates of the revolution were opened by the financial embarrassments of the government. The financial situation of the government must, however, not be confounded with the economical condition of the country. It was an audacious untruth when Necker asserted at the formal opening of the States-General, that the financial distress had by no means rendered it an imperative necessity to convene them. But it cannot be contested that, though the load was heavy, the economical resources of France were more than adequate to it. The whole subsequent history is one continuous proof of this assertion. That the *ancien régime* broke down under the weight, was entirely due to its not being properly distributed. Taxation under the *ancien régime* was in a very high degree governed by the principle: to whomsoever hath, shall be given more; and from whomsoever hath not, shall be taken what he hath.

This applies less to individuals than to the three estates forming, politically and socially, the constituent parts of the nation—the product of mediæval evolution. With the transformation of the feudal state the cleavage had in some respects become more complete. In a way the two upper estates underwent a process of consolidation, the class distinction getting tinged by an admixture of the caste principle; and, on the other hand, their vital principle became extinct. Their rights, which originally had had their proper correlate in corresponding duties, changed, by the gradual cessation of these duties, into privileges without any moral foundation. And the most prominent among these privileges was that of more or less extended tax-immunities.

In this respect the first estate or order, the "Clergy of France," constituted a homogeneous and compact whole. It was not wholly exempt from the public burdens, but its contributions did not correspond to the wealth of the church, and, besides, it depended to a great extent on its own free will how large they should be, while the mass of the people was taxed at discretion. The government had no right to impose any direct tax upon the clergy,[1] but every ten years its Ordinary Assembly voted the so-called *don gratuit*. I do not say granted, for although it is significantly termed a "*free gift*," it was in a sense acknowledged by the clergy to be obligatory. It was one of the innumerable cases in history where custom has acquired the force of law. By common consent a certain sum was considered the minimum, which the Ordinary Assembly was, though not legally, yet in duty bound to allow.[2] The government,

[1] This applies only to the "Clergy of France." The so-called "Foreign Clergy" of the eastern and northern provinces, which had been incorporated since the 16th century, was subject to some of the regular direct taxes. When in 1750 the government contemplated a breach into this privilege of the clergy of France, the bishops, convened in general assembly at Paris, wrote (Sept. 10) to the king: "*Nous ne consentirons jamais, que ce qui a été jusqu'ici le don de notre amour devienne le tribut de notre obéissance.*"

[2] Still, for 1789 the government received nothing, and for 1788 only 1,800,000*l*., while the yearly average during the reign of Louis XVI. was not quite four and a half millions.

however, was wont urgently to plead for more, and as to this Plus, the Assembly, though not turning a deaf ear to the appeals to its patriotism, was by no means inclined virtually to renounce the full discretion it could legally claim. It exercised this discretion not only by giving less than the government had asked. To attach conditions to its grants was no uncommon thing, and this was of much greater consequence. To the right of voting its own direct contributions and to the manner in which the opportunities offered by this right were improved, it is mainly due that the church by its official representation exercised at regular intervals a true political activity..

Though with the growing financial distress, naturally also the grumbling about these privileges of the clergy grew louder and more general, the animosity excited by them would not have become one of the most potent ferments, if they had been all which the people had to complain about on this score. They assumed such an exasperating character in the thought and feeling of the tax-ridden masses, because the church itself levied heavy and vexatious taxes upon them. In this respect the clergy also constituted in a measure a compact whole, for the humble parish priest had his share of the tithes too. That was, with the exception of his clerical character, about all he had in common with the higher church dignitaries, and with a great number of these the clerical character was only the means to gain access to the full bins of the church. The fat places of the church were as much as, if not more than ever, the ready means for providing for the younger sons and other needy members of the nobility,[1] very many of whom scorned even to pretend in the slightest degree that they had donned the clerical robe for any other purpose than to get the revenues of the rich abbacies and bishoprics. Yes, the church was rich,[2] but the lower clergy, principally in the rural

[1] About one-half of the whole income of the church went to the nobility. 19 chapters for men, 25 for women, and the 260 commanderies of the Maltesian Knights of St. John were by law exclusively reserved to it. Of the 1,500 ecclesiastical sinecures subject to royal appointment, they had virtually also the monopoly.—Mme. Campan, Mém., I. 237, writes : "Une autre décision de la cour qui ne pouvait être annoncée par un édit fut qu'à l'ávenir tous les biens ecclésiastiques depuis le plus modeste prieuré jusqu'aux plus riches abbayes, seraient l'apanage de la noblesse. Fils d'un chirurgien de village, l'abbé de Vermond, qui avait beaucoup de pouvoir dans tout ce qui concernait la feuille des bénéfices était pénétré de la justice de cette décision."

[2] It owned one-fifth to one-fourth of the soil, yielding an income of 80 to 100 millions. The whole income from

parishes, too often barely eked out a most miserable existence.¹ The position of the lower clergy—constituting of course an overwhelming majority—strikes one infinitely less as that of aristocrats lifted above the common crowd, than as that of proletarians in their own order—a fact which was to exercise a decisive influence on the course of the revolution in its first stages. On the other hand, the incumbents of the episcopal sees and great abbacies were the privileged of the privileged. So far as they chose, they unloaded the duties of their offices on other shoulders, and led a high life in their quality of feudal lords. This they all were in a large degree, and many in a much higher degree than almost all the secular lords. They all enjoyed the feudal emoluments and the minor, but to the people exceedingly burdensome feudal privileges, as that of the exclusive

---

invested property has been estimated at 124 millions. The tithes—about one-thirteenth of the gross products of the soil—amounted to about as much.

[1] On the 2d of Nov., 1789, the National Assembly voted upon Mirabeau's motion that every curacy should have an income of at least 1,200*l*. As the revolution at this time embraced with zeal the cause of the lower clergy against the high dignitaries of the church, one can infer from this sum what the income of many curacies must have amounted to before.—Œuvres, II. 327.

right of chase, which, to an incredible extent, put the fruits of the peasant's sweat at their tender mercies. Besides, many of them were in the main still the petty sovereigns they had originally been, endowed with strictly governmental prerogatives, including that of jurisdiction and the right of appointment.

Here is the point where sets in one of the most portentous delusions into which the revolutionary leaders were betrayed. On the one hand, there was manifestly deep resentment against the church in the masses, and on the other unbelief had made such inroads upon the clergy, that a contemporary writes: "A simple priest, a parson, must believe something, or he would be considered a hypocrite, but at the same time he must not be quite sure of what he believes, or else he would be considered intolerant. A grand-vicar may, however, smile a little over a sally against religion, a bishop laugh quite openly, and a cardinal even add himself some taunt." Now from these two facts the revolutionary leaders came to conclude that the Voltairian spirit, which imbued the great majority of the educated classes, had also pervaded the masses, and that their resentment was hatred of the Catholic Church as such, or even alienation from and contempt for the Christian religion. In truth they only hated the clergy in their quality of the most privileged class in regard to taxation, and of the most exacting among the feudal lords. Besides, even in judging the clergy from this point of view, the masses were not so utterly lost to all sense of justice as not to make some allowance for the fact, that after all, ninety out of a hundred were at least not mere drones.

In this respect the second order, the nobility, stood in a worse light. As nobility, it had no longer any political existence whatever. From a political order it had been entirely transformed into a privileged class. The way had been cleared for this baneful transformation by the changes wrought in the art of war, principally since the fourteenth century. In the first half of the sixteenth century it had been sedulously and dexterously furthered by Francis I. for political reasons, and Louis XIV. systematically and with consummate skill completed it.

The lower nobility, of course, continued to reside on its estates. If thrown into contact with the *bourgeoisie* in the provincial towns it was wont to point by haughty, if not positively insolent bearing to the gulf separating it from common mortals. Towards the peasants it was usually affable, ready to give good advice, and even to help. But from all public affairs it had been systematically crowded out by the administration, and it grew more and more to consider them beneath its dignity, because they were the domain of the government-clerks. It fairly prided itself upon not knowing anything about them. "To our order in particular," said Mirabeau on the eve of the revolution to the nobility of the Provence, " the reproach is addressed, that we want to decide everything without having learned anything."[1] Besides, an appalling percentage of it had become thoroughly impoverished. It had often to live upon the feudal emoluments,[2] and if so, it was in a way compelled to harden its heart against its liegemen. "Most of the fiefs," says Bouillé in his Memoirs,[3] " were in the hands of the *bourgeois* of the cities."

The great families, once powerful and often

[1] January 21, 1789, in the *assemblée des possédans-fiefs de Provence.*—Œuvres, I. 3.

[2] In the great night of Aug. 4, 1789, which swept feudalism out of France, the Duc d'Aiguillon deemed it necessary to call especial attention to this fact. "*Les droits . . . sont la seule fortune de plusieurs particuliers.*"—Archives Parlementaires, VIII. 344.

[3] P. 50.

turbulent vassals, were entirely reduced to the condition of an obsequious court nobility. I must leave its characterization in this quality for my next lecture. To-day we have to look at it from another point of view.

Absenteeism had become more and more the rule with the *grand seigneur*. The management of the estate was left to a bailiff, who grew fat and rich,[1] while the owner became poor, the estate deteriorated, and the peasant was more or less mercilessly sheared. While feudalism was still a live institution, the nobleman lived among his peasants, with them, and to a considerable degree, for them. In naïve primitiveness he had been their chief and their government. Therefore the peasant was attached to him, and willingly bore the burdens which a vigorous people is always ready to bear for the sustenance of its government. Now the moral ties that had bound them together were cut. All the obligations of the peasant were still in

---

[1] "*Les propriétaires des fiefs, des terres seigneuriales, ne sont, il faut l'avouer, que bien rarement coupables des excès dont se plaignent leurs vassaux ; mais leurs gens d'affaires sont souvent sans pitié, et le malheureux cultivateur, soumis au reste barbare des lois féodales qui subsistent encore en France, gémit de la contrainte dont il est la victime.*"
—Duc d'Aiguillon, Aug. 4, 1789, Arch. Parl., VIII. 344.

force, nay, partly they had become greater and partly the general change of conditions had rendered them more oppressive; but all the compensatory obligations of the lord had ceased. To this decisive point, I think, not all the weight that is due to it has been allowed by a distinguished American author in his excellent book on "The Eve of the French Revolution." In Germany feudalism was at the time partly even harsher than in France; but in this cardinal respect the German landed nobility compared very favorably with the French, and therefore the peasantry was much less embittered against it. In France the peasant often hardly ever saw his gracious lord, but over and above the rent he had to pay or the labor he had to do for him, he was made to feel his existence most sorely at every step. The game laws were models of galling injustice and cruelty. The peasant was not allowed to put up fences without permission, and that was not easily granted; a broad continuous strip of land had always to be left free for the hunt to pass. During the hatching season of the wild fowl he was forbidden to put a foot on his own meadows, and still more to cut any grass, even if his cattle starved. What deer and boars had not destroyed, was plundered by the pigeons, which the lord alone had a right to keep—surely not an indifferent matter, for the dove-cots contained up to 5,000 pairs. And when the crop was at last in the barn the vexations still went on. Now he was bidden when, another time where, and sometimes even at what price to sell. At the bridge over the brook the lord exacted a toll. What the peasant kept for his own use he had to cart to the manorial mill to be ground, and the flour to the manorial oven to be baked. Thus the change of conditions had perverted into an absurd and odious privilege what originally had been a kind service rendered by the lord to his tenantry. And the last-mentioned privilege is in yet another respect a most instructive illustration. If one wants to understand the intensity of the peasant's discontent, it is not sufficient to ascertain the absolute weight of the load he was made to carry. Its nature is of equal account—the How is as important as the How Much. He was goaded from the first to the last day of the year, and it is much easier to bear a short, sharp pain, than to keep one's temper under the infliction of a not very severe, but chronic toothache. Mr. Lowell is probably right in asserting that the condition of the rural classes in France " was better than that of the greater part of mankind,"[1] though, if the word "mankind" is to be understood literally, that is not saying very much, considering the position held by France in the world as to civilization and natural resources. Mirabeau's father is no mean authority on a question of this kind, and the picture he draws of the condition of the peasantry is dark enough. "Agriculture," he writes, "as practiced by our peasants, is a veritable galley-slavery; from their infancy they die by thousands, and in their youth they try to find a place anywhere but where they ought to be."[2] The less the wonder, for the peasant was subjected to all the smarting exactions and vexations solely because he happened to be born in a hovel and the nobleman in a castle. Is it astonishing that, in looking at this castle, the thought at last crept into his embittered heart to throw the incendiary's torch on its proud roof at the first good opportunity?

On the eve of the revolution the nobility, and in fact all the privileged classes, proved that the humanitarian spirit awakened and fostered by the great writers of the preceding epoch had taken a strong hold upon them and cast deep roots in their

[1] The Eve of the French Revolution, 206.
[2] Traité de la Population, 83.

minds. Taine is of opinion that "the aristocracy was never so worthy of power as at the moment it was going to lose it."[1] But it was too late. The same writer says: "Against all its natural chiefs, the men in office and invested with authority, the distrust of the people is inveterate and incurable. Their wishing it well and working for its welfare is of no use. It refuses to believe in their humanity and disinterestedness. It has been trodden down too much. It distrusts all measures coming from them, even the most salutary and liberal ones."[2]

Thus we see that, as to its relations to the peasantry, the effects of that transformation of the nobility had been altogether injurious to both parties. But possibly the nobility had a better showing to make, when judged as a class from the point of view of the whole commonwealth.

The feudal state had professed the principle, that the nobleman pays with his blood and the villein with his money. Did the first part of this maxim still hold good? In a sense, yes. The French nobility was still ever ready to shed as much of its blood as France required. But it was

---

[1] Les Origines de la France contemporaine, I. 392.
[2] Ib., I. 495.

no longer its duty to do so, and that made all the difference in the world. The duty had been perverted into a privilege. The commoner, who had a liking for military service, had to be satisfied with at best becoming a non-commissioned officer. Every commissioned officer was in a way a walking insult to nine-tenths of the nation, for the insignia of his rank cried in their faces: " Plebeians, remember that it is but base stuff that is coursing in your veins!" Besides, that a nobleman was a commissioned officer by no means of necessity implied that he at least really served. Only a little more than one-third of the officers were actively employed, and not being actively employed did not preclude promotion.

The nobility had thus not the shadow of a moral right to claim immunity from taxation on the strength of paying with its blood. Nor did its pretensions embrace that point. What it claimed as a matter of course was to pay less than its fair share, and that the *ancien régime* acknowledged to be its incontestable right. To the indirect taxes, from which about half of the revenue was derived, it was, of course, subjected like the rest of the people. But as these were principally laid upon articles of primary necessity, which are consumed more according to the capacity of one's stomach than to that of one's pocket, it paid proportionately infinitely less than the poor. From the majority of the direct taxes it was not exempted either, but it was very ingenious in discovering ways and means to have its proper quota reduced, and the higher in rank, the more consummate was the skill and shamelessness with which this low art was practiced. And, finally, from the *taille*, the direct tax which surpassed all others not only in amount, but also in vexatiousness, on account of the positively insane manner of its collection, it was wholly excused.[1]—Can one, in looking at this picture, accuse Rousseau of very gross exaggeration in his description of the pact the rich concludes with the poor : you shall have the honor of serving me, and as a consideration for the honor of being commanded by me, you shall give me the little you have ?

And the picture is by far not yet complete. To pay the *taille* alone and unassisted was not the

---

[1] The exemption attached to the estate and not to the owner. But while, as I mentioned, many commoners had become the owners of noble estates, the converse was, for obvious reasons, so rare a case that it is substantially correct to say that the landed proprietor of noble extraction was exempted from paying the *taille*.

only privilege of the masses. They had also the monopoly of the *corvée*, the road service ; they alone could boast of the proud distinction to have to serve in the militia ; they alone had the honor of having soldiers quartered on them. They appreciated these prerogatives the more, because not only the clergy and nobility, but also all who were in their service, did not enjoy them.

The effect of all this upon the disposition of the masses was greatly intensified by the ingenuity the *ancien régime* displayed in rendering the unequal and unjust working of the tax-screw unnecessarily painful.

The indirect taxes were not levied directly by the government. Capitalists clubbed together and rented them for a number of years at a fixed sum. A considerable part of this was always paid in advance, but at an exorbitant rate of interest. They did the collecting and kept the product. That overstrained mercifulness was not the chief characteristic of their agents, goes without saying. The government aided them to the best of its ability to enhance the enormous profits of the Farmers-General by invariably allowing them the benefit of the doubt in cases of dispute between them and the taxpayers. Among the reforms effected by Turgot the reversal of this principle does not occupy the last place.

And even this does not yet give us anything like an adequate conception of the working of the tax system. One feature of it, to which I have already alluded in quite a general way—the inequality of the provinces—calls for an ampler illustration. The *gabelle*, the salt-tax, serves our purpose best, because it is also in other respects eminently characteristic. Some provinces were wholly exempt from it; in others it was, comparatively speaking, more or less moderate; in some crushing. The difference in the price in the first and last category was at the ratio of one to thirteen. The tax was partly the highest in those very provinces which nature had supplied most abundantly with this indispensable necessary. Under severe penalties were the inhabitants of the coast forbidden to let their cattle drink the sea-water. To buy at least seven pounds of salt annually for every member of the household over seven years of age was obligatory, and these seven pounds must be used exclusively for cooking purposes and on the table. Woe to him who dared to salt a piece of meat with it for use in the winter, or, even in a case of pressing emergency, ventured to boil a few ounces out of the brine in his herring-cask. Two years before the outbreak of the revolution Calonne had, in an official report, the following story to tell about the consequences of this glorious tax-device of this most paternal government: 4,000 seizures, 3,400 imprisonments, 500 sentences to whipping, exile, and the galleys—*annually*. What an admirable contrivance to breed and educate a class of hardened, habitual law-breakers! How well those, who had been through this school—and the *ancien régime* had half a dozen of equal efficacy—would know how to lead in the dance, when a political revolution opened the flood-gates to a social revolution, ushering in a day of reckoning, when the masses had it in their power to square all old accounts!

Calonne's figures give us a glimpse of the darkest cloud that was hovering over the future of France. The masses of the French people were, under the *ancien régime*, as laborious and as frugal as they are to-day. That they were exceedingly far from being then as thrifty as they are now, was solely the fault of the iniquities and follies of the political and social system that weighed them down. But direful as its effects upon their economical condition were, they were the least part of the harm wrought by it. Mr. Lowell says: "The peasant's taxes were constantly getting heavier, but his means of bearing them increased faster yet. The rising tide of material prosperity, the great change of modern times, could be felt, though feebly as yet, in the provinces of France." I do not contest the fact, and the same unquestionably holds good—even in a higher degree—of the city population. But from the political point of view this was irrelevant, or only aggravated the situation. Mr. Lowell very correctly says in another place: "It is in their decrepitude that political abuses are most ferociously attacked." In this case the resentment against them grew not only with their progressing decrepitude, but was besides fanned by the relative improvement in the economical condition of the masses, for it necessarily opened their eyes more and more to the fact how glaring the abuses were, and made them more and more impatient of bearing them any longer.[1]

There was the more danger in this, because to a considerable extent what Taine says of the peasantry also holds good of the masses in the cities:

---

[1] Taine sums up the facts in the brief sentence: "The more the peasant acquires and produces, the heavier his burdens become."—I. 445.

"They thought *en blocs*," *i. e.*, in lumps. It is perhaps still more correct to say, they did not really think at all, but merely jumped at conclusions, their smarting flesh constituting the premises. What that signified the course of the revolution was to make terribly clear. When they commenced to formulate their conclusions—they had not even done that, as long as it had seemed to them that the yoke was grown fast to their neck—it was vain to appeal to their reason. They had none and could have none as to the questions at issue. Their only guides were the heart-burnings of the past, the passions of the present, and bewitching mirages of an impossible future—products of imagination lashed into delirium by excitement, and unrestrained by either experience or trust in any recognized authority. Then it became fearfully apparent that distrust of, and bitterness against the government required but an opportunity to crysstallize into the mad notion, that in the nature of things government is and always must be the enemy of the people. And then it became as fearfully apparent, that the dangers springing from the financial difficulties were but as dust in the scales compared to those arising from the social and moral disintegration of the people wrought by the *ancien régime* with the privilege-corrosive. The economic effects of the iniquities and follies of the political and social system furnished only the occasion for the formal initiation of the revolution. Its real causes were their moral effects. Therefore these determined its character and course. Von Sybel is unquestionably right: "The deepest wound of France was the hostile discord between the different classes of the people."

The worst, however, was not the depth of the wound. If it had been a clean cut the skillful political surgeon would have found it only a grave, but not a desperate case. But the flesh was lacerated, and not blood, but putrid matter, oozed from it in profusion. The poisoning of the blood caused by it made the wound fatal.

What of it, if the peasant had to live as much for the lord as for himself, because he happened to be born in a hovel and the nobleman in a castle? In the eyes of the nobility that was no more an accident, than that the king owed the crown to the accident of his birth. Is there any sense in calling it an accident, that sparrows are not hatched in the hawk's and the eagle's nest, and *vice versa?* These gentlemen saw no flaw in the simile. They were thoroughly honest believers in the doctrine of blue blood, and understood it quite literally. In 1614 the States-General had been convened for the last time. The representatives of the third estate called themselves on this occasion, in the address they read to the king, the younger sons of the common mother France. The nobility demurred against this as an insult, declaring it an unwarranted pretension, because members of the third estate "were neither of the same blood nor of the same virtue." The difficulty to maintain the theory, which prompted the insolent rebuke, of course increased with the additions made by the government to the old nobility of the sword. Had the money, which was paid for offices conferring nobility, the magic force instantly to change the color and composition of the blood? Certainly an awkward question, which it was easier to shove aside than to answer. But it was not quite so embarrassing as it might appear at first sight. Though the whole nobility had blue blood, the intensity of the blueness greatly varied. How tenaciously those who were blessed with the higher grades stuck to this maxim, and how well they understood how to turn it to good account, is proved by the curious and significant fact, that even in the last years before the revolution, the army regulations were made much more stringent in this respect. Even to obtain a commission as second lieutenant one had to be from 1781, on the father's side, a nobleman at least in the fourth generation. Thus, even by being ennobled, one is by no means directly lifted out of the category of mere mortals; only in the fourth generation does one become a real man—and then not much of a one. Voltaire was thrown into the Bastille, because he had the presumption to call to account a noble brute, that had done him the honor to have him caned by his lackeys; but then a petition presented by the peers in 1717 to the Duke-Regent had insisted upon it, that they should not be obliged to accept a challenge from simple noblemen, "even if they have been caned." So the distance between a peer and a common nobleman is deemed as great as that between the nobleman and —to use the significant term of the times—people "without birth."

The other privileges claimed in this famous petition are quite in keeping with this one. Only from the hands of a bishop will the peers receive the sacrament; they alone are to have cushions at church; at banquets their health shall be drunk before that of the host and hostess; in the theatres and in driving on the streets they are to have precedence, "in spite of all inconveniences this might lead to;" artisans shall have no right to invoke the aid of the courts to make them pay their debts —they shall only be allowed to remind them of it, "but not often." Does one not feel stifled in the mummy-air exhaled by such precious parchments from the archives of the *ancien régime!*

But we must beware of being unjust towards the stars circling around the royal sun. The same spirit pervades the *bourgeoisie*, and there it is the more repellent, because not marquises and dukes, but plain Mr. Shoemaker and Mr. Barber knock their noses bloody against the sun. An intendant reports: "At last it has been decided that the *présidial* is to have the holy-water presented before the members of the city council. The Parliament hesitated. The king himself decided the question. It was high time. This affair threw the whole city into commotion." And so it is all over. The office-selling has carried the nefarious spirit everywhere, for, even to the lowliest office, some nonsensical little privilege attaches, and that is defended as if life and salvation depended on it. Everywhere, vanity struts in its most despicable forms. There was not only hostile discord between the three orders, but the bane of privilege had eaten itself so deeply into all the social layers, that society almost seemed dissolved into its elements. Therefore all attempts to repress the evil within bounds had to prove futile. *Sit ut est, aut non sit,*—continue to be as it is, or cease to exist,—that was the stern decree of the logic of facts. To eliminate the privilege-principle from the political and social system was, however, in itself the radical destruction of the *ancien régime*. But by letting privilege more and more become its very essence, so that one could be tempted to characterize its once proud structure as all rotten props and no walls, the *ancien régime* not merely wrought its own ruin. The wanton excess, to which the iniquitous privilege-fatuity was carried in all its forms, begot the inexorable levelling spirit of the revolution, sparing nothing, and adopting, to make sure of its work, the never-failing methods of Procrustes.

If any one had no right to pass judgment upon the spirit that ruled France from 1793 to 1795, it was the champion of the *ancien régime*. This spirit was the legitimate offspring of the political and social system bequeathed by Louis XIV. and Louis XV. to Louis XVI.

LECTURE II.

Paris and Versailles.

THE man who understood the revolution better than any other actor in it—whose unique political instinct intuitively divined it, whenever even his equally phenomenal political reasoning powers were baffled by the veils enshrouding its awful mysteries—said: " Paris is the sphinx of the Revolution, but I shall tear her secret from her." [1] If Mirabeau ever afterwards directly asserted, that he had completely succeeded in doing so, I have never heard of it. But, however that be, the historian of the revolution, in whom this confession of its most penetrating intellect does not awaken some diffidence, is blessed with infinitely more self-confidence than I can boast of. Still, however inadequate my powers be, I must draw you

---

[1] Passy, Frochot, 72.—See the anything but attractive picture of Paris sketched by Mirabeau in the Lettres de Cachet, I. 254.

in the few minutes at my disposal a sketch of the sphinx, ere she arises in all her might; for one thing is certain: the history of the revolution can no more be understood without understanding the part played in it by Paris, than one can conceive of the tragedy of Hamlet with the part of Hamlet left out; and to understand the part played by Paris in the revolution without knowing the Paris before the revolution is equally impossible.

The difficulty in getting at the secret of the sphinx lies in this, that she had several heads and several hearts, each with ideas, impulses, aspirations, sentiments, and passions of its own, constantly running athwart each other, now this and now that—really or apparently—ruling the day or the hour; and yet she is one, always throwing the tremendous weight of the whole into the scales.

Let us commence at the bottom with the nobodies. They are no specialty of Paris. There are many of them in every city, but the larger the city the greater the percentage. Paris, therefore, has the highest. They are isolated particles. In the ushering in of the new era they have no part. The regulations concerning the elections to the States-General contain no provision in regard to them. That their existence was actually forgotten, can hardly be supposed, though there is no telling, whether the men who still presided over the destinies of France were not even equal to that. It was simply a matter of course, that these nobodies went for nothing in the question at hand. Whether they were likely to continue to be nothing in it, nobody seems to have asked. They were isolated particles, but of the highest imaginable affinity. A little heat would convert them into a solid mass, and the weight of this would tell—law or no law permitting it to get into the scales.

The existence of this class was partly due to natural causes, the working of which the wit of man can to a degree mitigate, but never prevent. In the *ancien régime*, however, the wit of man had altogether been bent upon stimulating it. The privilege-bane had also been extended over the domain of labor. When, in 1776, Turgot broke down the guilds, the Parliament of Paris strenuously opposed the government, declaring: all Frenchmen are divided into established corporations, forming one continuous chain from the throne down to the lowest handicraft, indispensable to the existence of the state, and not to be abolished, lest the whole social order break asunder. That was but too true. Since the days of Henry III. (1574–89) the forcing of all industrial pursuits into the strait-jacket of guildships had been carried to the extreme of utter absurdity. Here, too, the chronic financial distress had been the principal cause. At first the handicrafts, which everybody had been at liberty to practice, were withdrawn from free competition and sold as a privilege, and then, when nothing was left to be sold, the old guilds were split up into a number of guildlets, merely to have again something to put on the counter. And it was not only left pretty much to the masters whom they would admit to the freedom of the guild, but besides the charges for it were so high, that it was often absolutely out of the reach even of the most skillful journeyman. Even a blood-aristocracy was not lacking. In a number of guilds only the sons of masters and the second husbands of masters' widows could become masters. Thus an immense proletariat was gradually formed, which to a great extent was a proletariat only because the law irresistibly forced it into this position. And the city proletariat proper received constant and ever-increasing additions from the country.

There such distress prevailed, that the paupers flocked in crowds to the cities, hoping that there it would be easier, in some way or other, by hook or by crook, to eke out some kind of an existence. The curious and highly-important fact, that, in spite of emigration and the general prostration of business, the population of Paris grew throughout the revolution more rapidly than ever before,[1] is only the intensified and accelerated development of a characteristic social phenomenon of the *ancien régime*. What this kind of growth signified can be inferred from the fact that in 1791, long before the inauguration of the Reign of Terror, there were in a population of 650,000, 118,000 paupers (*indigents*).[2] Under the *ancien régime* the immigrant proletariat from the country was by the law barred out from all ways of earning a livelihood except as common day-laborers, and the wages of these were in 1788, on an average, 26 cents for men and 15 for women, while the price of bread was higher than in our times. What a gigantic heap of ferment! Was it to be presumed, that the resentment accumulated through

---

[1] The growth has been estimated at 150,000.

[2] As early as March 16, 1790, Bailly, at the time mayor of Paris, told the National Assembly: "Depuis six mois le peuple de Paris ne vit que d'aumônes."

generations in these masses would all turn into the milk of gratitude, when the law itself suddenly battered a wide breach into the legal walls, which so cruelly had hemmed them in? Or was it more likely, that a terrific explosion would ensue? What would be more in conformity with human nature as it really is—especially where education has done nothing, or next to nothing, to provide intellectual or moral bonds to restrain the original beast slumbering in the human breast—cannot be doubtful. Here educational influences of the opposite tendency had been vigorously exerted. The law-abiding spirit of the masses was systematically undermined. It is another of the high-schools of the *ancien régime* for training habitual law-breakers, and they went unpunished because they were far too numerous to render punishment possible. They are embittered against the government; there is, when they begin to think about it, in the existing conditions of things nothing that is dear to them; the very fact of their being a vast mass renders them excitable; when the blood of a few is stirred, that of all instantly begins to course faster in their veins, and the heightened temperature of every one reacts upon that of the whole mass; a single burning straw can easily be put out by a child, but if it be one of a huge pile the burning candle cannot with impunity be held to it; they do not reason, but they feel all the more intently; they will follow every voice striking the tone, which, at the moment, awakens a responsive echo in their breasts, and they have not been taught in vain not to scruple to take the law into their own hands; and finally, in an upheaval, which would turn everything topsy-turvy, they had nothing to lose, but everything to gain. In a revolution resorting to force, every demagogue would find in them the flying columns ever ready to his hands, and in a revolution coming to believe revolution in itself the magic panacea for all political and social evils and dangers, it would be the easiest thing in the world to work them into a mental and moral delirium stopping short at absolutely nothing.

For the present, however, they were to such a degree an inert mass that the *bourgeoisie* ignored them as completely as the government. That rendered bad worse. If you know you have a cask of powder in your cellar, you will be careful not to go near it with fire. If your contemptuous indifference to the foul and unsightly stuff goes to the extent of not ascertaining its nature, you won't mind putting the burning candle right into it. That the *bourgeoisie* did. It never dreamed of the possibility, that some day its texts might be appropriated by the proletariat of the suburbs of St. Antoine and St. Marceau to preach a sermon upon in its own way. As the Marquise du Chatelet, Voltaire's friend, saw no reason why she should not make her whole toilet in the presence of her footmen, as a lady of her rank could not possibly consider this *canaille* real *men*, thus it never occurred to the *bourgeoisie* to inquire whether the heads and hearts of the proletarians really were such utterly barren sands, that its ideas, complaints, and aspirations could by any possibility ever germ and take root in them.

It is true, the hotter its contest with the *ancien régime* waxed, the less the *bourgeoisie* objected to being occasionally applauded by the proletarians; and when experience had taught it the effect of their applause, it was quick to learn to provoke it. Only according to its programme, they were, as a matter of course, merely to serve as a *claque*, dutifully waiting for the signal. That the proletarians would, at least as a rule, for a while do so, was not at all improbable. Quite certain, however, it was that when the *bourgeoisie* had carried its points with their help, they would not heed its cry of "Halt, enough!" They were absolutely sure then not only to continue the fight against the common adversaries of old, but also to turn against the *bourgeoisie* itself, for they had to settle an account with it, that was of as old a date as that with the government and the privileged classes, and not much lower in amount either. A few weeks after the insurrection of the 31st of May, 1793, by which the Jacobins put their heels upon the Girondists, Robespierre wrote : " The internal dangers come from the *bourgeois;* to vanquish the *bourgeois* the people must be rallied. All measures had been taken to force the yoke of the *bourgeoisie* upon the people. . . . The present insurrection must be continued until all measures have been taken to save the republic. . . . Pursuant to the same plan the insurrection must be carried from city to city, the *sans-culottes* must be paid, stay in the cities, and receive arms." [1] We, before whose eyes the whole field lies spread out, can see with the utmost clearness, that nothing could avert the day when these lines would be penned. In the relations between the *bourgeoisie* and the proletariat under the *ancien régime* the finger of fate had

[1] E. Hamel: Histoire de Robespierre, III. 72.

irrevocably written the decree, that after they had jointly drowned the monarchy in blood, the proletariat would consider it as sacred a duty to crush the *bourgeoisie* even more mercilessly.

The disintegrating tendencies of the *ancien régime* were at work in the cities with full force. Turgot complained: " Every city, exclusively devoted to its own interests, is inclined to sacrifice to them the estates and villages of its district." And within the cities the public interests sickened under the load of the innumerable special interests created or fostered by the *ancien régime,* and every class was nearly as exclusively devoted to its own interests. As to the guild-fetters, at least half of the responsibility and blame unquestionably attached to the *bourgeoisie.* Nor did it stop at keeping free competition shut out by the law. Like the two upper orders, it everywhere managed to throw the bulk of the public burdens upon the masses below them, partly by acquiring some petty office, carrying with it some exemption from taxation, partly by making the *octroi, i. e.,* the excises, or consumption taxes, the principal income-source of the city.

When, with the annihilation of the enemy in front, the ally in the rear changed into a mortal enemy, it became apparent that, by breaking up into numberless groups and grouplets crystallizing around some petty selfish interest, the *bourgeoisie* had erected its own scaffold and dug its own grave. There is not a day in the revolution when the *bourgeoisie* could not have put an end to terroristic radicalism. Nothing can be further from the truth than to think that in Paris, or anywhere in France, the majority of the people became victims to the epidemic mania of terrorism. The deeper Paris, and with Paris, France, is plunged into the despotism of bloody anarchy, the smaller is the number of those by whom the country allows itself to be held in an infernal vice. This is proved beyond the possibility of contradiction by the returns of election after election. The solution of the riddle, which contains the main-key to the second phase of the revolution, can be given in six words: there is no longer a *bourgeoisie*. Only *bourgeois* are left, and every one of them acted upon the maxim of Siéyès, who, when asked what he had done during the reign of terror, laconically replied : " *J'ai vécu,*"—I lived. Upon the " Everybody-take-care-of-himself " of the *bourgeois* frightened out of their manhood, the terrorists reared their power.

Looking at the *bourgeoisie* of the *ancien régime* and especially of Paris from the opposite point of view, not only a more pleasing, in fact a very attractive picture presents itself. The pulse of life is vigorously throbbing in its veins, and it is a life manifestly auguring a better future for the whole country. Thanks to its steady application, ingenuity, and enterprise, the material condition of all its layers has greatly improved and continues to improve, despite all the artificial impediments of the *ancien régime*. With growing prosperity all social amenities and refinements of life are better appreciated, and the intellectual life powerfully stimulated. Many of the foremost intellectual pathfinders of the 18th century come from its ranks, and many a grain from their ample seed-pouches finds a grateful soil even in its lower strata. The consequences of all this cannot easily be over-estimated. In spite of the countless artificial barriers, the social layers are undergoing an astounding levelling process. The upper classes voluntarily and involuntarily step down several rounds of the ladder, while the *bourgeoisie*, by the acquisition of wealth, knowledge, and social polish, climbs up at least as many. The distinctions of rank continue to be embroidered on the coats, but they more and more cease to be engraved in the thought and feeling. The shell of the old order of things still stood erect, but the moral principle which had constituted its vitality was dead.[1] The *bourgeoisie* not only thinks itself as good as the two upper orders, but in the consciousness of the worth of its labor it comes to deem itself even better than they. On the eve of the revolution, Siéyès directly declared: " The Third Estate comprises everything constituting the nation, and

[1] I cannot refrain from quoting in this connection a letter of Mirabeau's uncle written forty years before the revolution. "Je connais Paris ; sois sûr que cette vile populace qui y croupit, ou qui vient y croupir, pour y chercher fortune, comme si fortune était un chien perdu, est aussi corrompue que Rome lorsqu'elle chercha à détruire jusqu'au nom des patriciens ; compte que cet infâme peuple de parvenus qui donne le ton, soit dans la robe, soit dans la finance, est vraiment un peuple républicain par l'insolence, en même temps qu'indigne de l'être à cause de ses vices sans vertus. Quand un peuple en délire veut attaquer une monarchie, il commence toujours par la religion. Alors plus de prestiges ; bientôt la différence que Dieu lui-même a mise entre les hommes par les distinctions, dont nous voyons la première trace dans la législation des Juifs, paraît une injustice à ce peuple. Il sape la noblesse ; et le chef de la hiárarchie, dénué des appuis naturels de son trône, le sent ébranlé, et vacille dans sa place sacrée. Crois-tu qu'il y ait du remède? Je ne le crois pas, et voici pourquoi : c'est que la distinction entre la noblesse et la plebée n'est que morale et de convention ; on détruit cette distinction, et la noblesse est réduite à dé vaines prétentions qui les rendent pire qu'inutile."
—Mém., III. 193, 194.

whatever is not the third estate cannot consider itself as being of the nation." [1]

Notice that the writer of this sentence, which, if logically carried out in practice, would be in the fullest sense of the term a *radical* political and social revolution, was himself an *abbé*, a member of the first order. This points to a most important fact. The population of Paris did not consist merely of the *bourgeoisie* and the proletariat. The two upper orders were also largely represented in it, and most of them stood neither socially nor intellectually aloof. Constantly and in every respect were they in the closest touch with the uppermost strata of the *bourgeoisie*, and very many of them were among the most ardent and most influential votaries of the new ideas and new tendencies, which more and more pervaded the whole intellectual and moral life of the nation. These members of the two upper orders stood for a great deal in making Paris what it was; [2] and that Paris

---

[1] Qu'est-ce que le Tiers-Etat? p. 41, Edition Chapuys-Montlaville. Paris, 1839. Thus Taine's assertion (I. 424) is the literal truth : "The Third Estate says, like Louis XIV., '*L'Etat c'est moi.*'"

[2] To these elements, their direct and indirect influence, it was due to a great extent that, as Mirabeau wrote (June 16, 1790) to David Leroy, "Paris ne fut jamais, sous le despotisme, qu'une obstruction du corps politique, également

was what it was, was the most terrible of all the terrible dangers of the impending revolution.

Paris was not yet the commercial emporium of France, but in the most essential respects it was, even in a much higher degree than to-day, France herself. For a while it had been favored and fostered by the kings. Soon, however, its rapid growth began to alarm them. Ordinance upon ordinance trying to check this growth was issued, but they always proved utterly futile: one of the most drastic among the many illustrations of the complete impotence of paternal absolutism in contending against the development marked out by the nature and force of the actual conditions. Paris continued to grow, and the more it grew, the more it became the absorbing centre of everything constituting a determining and creative force in a nation's life. For talent and ambition of every variety, aspiring to more than a third-rate part, there was but one place in France, Paris. As early as 1740, Montesquieu wrote: "There is in France nothing but Paris and the distant provinces; the latter only because Paris has as yet not had time to

propre et destinée à le vampirer et à le corrompre."—Mém., VIII. 5.

swallow them." And the keen English observer, Arthur Young, who left Paris a few days before the storming of the Bastille, reports that there the press was in feverish activity; besides the newspapers, as many as 92 pamphlets were published in one week. In the provinces, however, hardly any pamphlets, and only very few newspapers, were printed. In the provinces there had been more and larger printing establishments in the 17th century than there were in the 18th, while, of course, infinitely more printing was done in France in the 18th than in the 17th century. Paris had monopolized the business of manufacturing the intellectual food for France. Small wonder, therefore, that Young meets with nothing but diffident silence. Whenever he propounds any political question, he invariably receives the exasperating answer: We are only a provincial city; we must wait and see what Paris will say and do. Paris alone really lived, but Paris knew only Paris. As to how things looked beyond its immediate surroundings, its notions were of the haziest sort. But that gave it little concern. As in regard to many questions of equal import, it drew a check upon its vivid imagination to make up for its lack of knowledge and judgment. The rest of

France is not lifeless, but it has not an independent life of its own. The initiative always and in every respect emanates from the focus on the Seine, and therefore the life of the provincials is in the main only a reflex. To say that the provinces only vegetated, would, however, in so far be wholly incorrect, as with dependence morbid sensitiveness to any impulse from Paris had grown apace. Especially in the principal provincial centres the intellectual and moral conditions were such, that, if the impulse from Paris attained an excessive degree of momentum, the reaction might easily even surpass it, if not in potency, at least in vehemence. That opened an appalling vista, in case a future was in store for France, whose signature was *storm*. As early as 1750, Mirabeau's father sententiously remarked in regard to the position Paris held in France: if the head grows too large, and all the blood courses towards it, the body becomes apoplectic. How then, if a day were to come when the supreme legal authorities would be compelled virtually to strike the flag before Paris, and that proletariat in the suburbs of St. Antoine and St. Marceau would speak the decisive word in the city? Then this proletariat would actually be the heart propelling the blood through the veins of the whole body politic, for the will of Paris was the law of France.

That in times of great political and social commotion fearful dangers would be conjured up by this abnormal position of Paris, was all the more certain, because here only the fermenting *new* ideas and tendencies had their creative centre. The pulsating heart of the *old* France was not there, but at such close proximity, that if Paris should ever become of opinion that its beating was altogether too much out of time, even women might not deem it too fatiguing to walk the distance for the purpose of giving it a regulating squeeze.

In Versailles the whole life of the *ancien régime* is legally and actually focused. Versailles even claims to be the France of the *ancien régime*. Speaking of great court days, it is the customary phrase with the writers, who are a part of Versailles, to say: "All France was present." And the whole life of this whole France concentrated there in the artificial creation of Louis XIV. is also in its turn legally and actually focused. "What of it," says Taine, "that Versailles has 80,000 inhabitants, is one of the biggest cities of the kingdom: it is filled, peopled, occupied, by the life of a single man."[1] That is no exaggeration, and it was so not primarily and principally because France was an absolute monarchy and the centre of the governmental apparatus was located at the king's habitual residence. Prussia was also an absolute monarchy under Frederick the Great, but we see nothing like it either in Potsdam or Berlin. The unique character of Versailles is due infinitely less to the fact that it is the seat of government, than to the further fact that it is the permanent residence of the court. Frederick the Great reigned and governed, reducing his holding of court to the absolutely indispensable. Louis XIV. also reigned and governed, but nevertheless made holding of court the first and paramount task and duty of the kings of France. When the etiquette of the French court was explained to Frederick the Great, he sarcastically remarked, that, if he had happened to be king of France, the first thing he would have done after his accession to the throne, would have been to appoint a king-adjunct to hold court for him. Indeed, recourse to some such measure would have been a necessity for a man of his stamp, for the French kings had to husband their time

[1] I. 103.

well to spare two or two and a half hours a day for state affairs.

Louis XIV. was fully conscious of what he was doing, when—although he fully lived up to his declaration at Mazarin's death, that henceforth he would be himself his prime minister—he made court-keeping the foremost state affair. He liked to hear himself called by his courtiers, "*le Roi Soleil,*"—the king-sun. They knew that the most extravagant flattery would be well received by him, and their servility was equal to driving it to the very acme of absurdity. "Sire, the rain of Versailles does not make wet," said one of them, with a profound reverence, when the king was overtaken by a shower in his promenade and gave permission to the suite to cover their heads. But Louis XIV. knew better than any one of the courtiers, that this appellation was not merely a flattering metaphor. As to them it strictly corresponded to the facts. It had been his conscious and set purpose to make himself the sun, around which they, as planets of all conceivable magnitudes, had to circle, receiving their motion and their light only from it, and to an astonishing degree he had succeeded in carrying out his intention.

The high nobility is expected to make Versailles

as much as possible its regular abode. The intendants are required to give in their official reports full information as to whether the nobility of their *généralité* is inclined or disinclined to do so. If the noblemen will not, or, for some reason or other, cannot comply with this wish of his majesty, a high moral pressure is brought to bear upon them, to come at least from time to time to Versailles to make their obeisance. Even a man of the standing of the old marshal of France, Rosen, has to undergo every year the fatigues of the journey from distant Alsace, solely for the purpose of fulfilling this duty. To attach oneself so far to the court that one comes to be considered a regular member of it, is to make one's nest in a golden cage,[1] even if one does not hold any office

---

[1] The closest compartment of it was, however, occupied by the king himself. Louis XVI. was very far from enjoying court-keeping. If it had been possible, he probably would have very willingly acted upon the suggestion of Frederick the Great to appoint a king-adjunct for this purpose. But the chains forged by the King-Sun for his successors were riveted so fast, that this absolute ruler over twenty-five millions could not even help making a perfect fool of himself. He did venture now and then to go in the early morning to Trianon, there to breakfast with Marie Antoinette, but all the while carefully watching the hands of the clock. Stern duty bade him be back at Versailles in time to undress and go back into his bed for the purpose of getting out of it again and being dressed once more with all the pomp and circumstance prescribed by the rules of 1681.

5

imposing any real or nominal duties. Not to assist at any of the daily ceremonies one has the right to attend, smacks of neglecting one's moral obligations. To indulge frequently in this kind of absenteeism is sure to be noticed, sooner or later, and when noticed, will cause more or less of an eclipse of the royal sun. Courtiers, therefore, are slow to leave Versailles for any length of time without asking the king's gracious consent, and this they do not venture to request very often. As a rule, however, they are only too glad to stay. What have the provincial cities to offer in comparison to Versailles and Paris? And their estates—if they have any—are duller still. Unless it be to hunt for a month or two, the thought of visiting them is usually far from being attractive, for it is wont to be associated with the vision of empty pockets imperatively demanding a more or less protracted season of recuperation.

Yes, not only amusement and excitement of every kind and the allurements offered to ambition make the court a magnet of almost irresistible force to whomsoever has once come within its sphere of attraction. The exact number of courtiers—female as well as male—who were tied to it as fast by their pockets, could hardly be figured out. But nothing would be easier than to prove that the percentage was very great, and the tendency constantly to become greater still very strong. The example which the *Roi Soleil* set in leading a life as if every night a dry rain of gold drizzled down upon the park of Versailles, was not lost upon his courtiers, and they ruined themselves as effectually as he the state; and the sons and grandsons were fully up to the mark of their sires. " With the exception of two or three hundred at the most," says Bouillé, "the old families were ruined. Most of the large titled estates had become the appanage of the financiers, merchants, and their descendants."[1] It was *bon ton*, not only to keep the serene and graceful smile on one's lips when the last *louis-d'or* was gone and the creditors refused to add any more entries in their ledgers to the already endless list, but also to pretend not to know the first thing about the condition of one's money affairs. "Sire," replied, blandly smiling, a prelate, whom the king asked whether the report was true that he

---

[1] According to Rabaut Saint-Etienne about one-fourth of the soil was still owned by the nobility. "On ne risquerait pas de se tromper en portant à un milliard le produit réel de la propriété foncière; pour plus de certitude, nous le réduirons à 800 millions, dont 200 millions possédés par la noblesse, au-delà de 110 millions par le clergé, et le surplus par le tiers-état."—A la nation française, 62.

was being hunted down by the importunities of his creditors, "I shall inquire of my bailiff and then report." But so much sound business instinct these fine folks possessed after all, to know full well that it is better to have something than nothing, and more than less, and neither *bon ton* nor their keen sense of honor were the slightest barrier to their applying—in season and out of season—to the king to turn on his big stop-cock, whether their own cask had run empty or not. Nor did the king see anything out of the way in this. The vaults of the state's treasury were practically his personal strong-box, so far as he chose to put them to this use; and it was but fair that, if he wanted to have his planets, he should also, without niggardly stinting, do his proper share to supply them with this indispensable element of motive-power.

It would be a great mistake to attribute solely to the passion of the kings for pomp and ostentation the incredible figures to which their retinue swelled in the course of time. As to the state, innumerable offices were created for the purpose of selling them; as to the court, innumerable offices were created for the purpose of paying courtiers for being courtiers. Two illustrations will suffice to prove this. A number of officials had to serve only three months in the year, so that there were four incumbents of the same office and four salaries had to be paid; and other offices need only be named to show that they belonged to this category, as, for instance, the "wine-runners" and the "hasteners of roasts." Is it, under such circumstances, so very astonishing, that, even after the considerable reductions of 1775 and 1776, the retinue of the king still numbered 9,050 persons, that the court swallowed up one-tenth of the whole revenue of the state, that even after the so-called "great reform of the mouth" of 1780, *Mesdames*, the daughters of Louis XV., three old spinsters, received 600,000*l*. for their table expenses, the queen four millions for hers, the two brothers of the king 8,300,000 for theirs, not counting the two millions from the crown-estates allotted to them?[1] On the other hand, is it so very astonishing, that, the court requiring such enormous sums, in 1753 the lackeys had not received their salaries for three years and the royal hostlers went a-begging at night, or that in 1778, 792,620*l*. were due to the wine-purveyor, and almost three and a half millions to the purveyor of fish and meat?

[1] Taine, I. 91.

Real and nominal offices were not the only means of mending the rickety fortunes of the courtiers. Direct presents of money were made, especially in the form of permanent pensions, which were often granted for no other reason than that the persons applying for them were favorites, or had an influential backing, and liked to spend more money than they had. "It is time to remember," says Mirabeau bluntly in his thirteenth Note to the court, " that the prostitution of the favors (*grâces*) and the disorder of the finances have undermined the throne and necessitated the revolution."[1] These pensions were granted without any reference to the condition of the treasury and made payable at all sorts of offices collecting revenue of some kind or other, but dispensing what they collected and running their accounts more or less independently of the treasury. The consequence was, that nobody knew exactly to how much the pensions amounted in the aggregate. At the time of Necker's first ministry they had run up to about 28 millions.[2]

[1] Corresp., II. 115.
[2] Two instances will sufficiently show how well the reasons for which the pensions were granted could stand the test. The Marquis d'Antichamp received four pensions : (1) "for the services of his late father;" (2) "for the same object"

Despite the reckless lavishness, with which the earnings of the tax-payers were thus conveyed into the pockets of the courtiers, the demand far exceeded the supply, so the tax-farmers were induced to step in and make up for the shortcomings of the government. To secure the pretended or real influence of courtiers the tax-farmers let them partake of their profits. This was called *croupes*. No man or woman, no matter how high in rank, blushed to let everybody know it, if he or she had the good fortune to be a *croupier*. Why should they? Did not their gracious master Louis XV.—the whole people talked about it—stand in the front rank of grain speculators, while grim famine held sway in more than one province of his kingdom? Small wonder that he saw no objection to issuing formal patents for a share in the *croupes*.

Here we have in a nutshell the outcome of Louis XIV.'s successful effort to make the holding

(*objet*); (3) "for the same reasons" (*raisons*); (4) "for the same causes" (*causes*). Degalois de la Tour was the happy recipient of three pensions: (1) "as first president and intendant;" (2) "as intendant and first president;" (3) "for the same above-mentioned reasons." According to R. Stourm, Les Finances de l'ancien Régime et de la Révolution, II. 134, the pensions even amounted to 32 millions, but of these only six to seven millions were granted without good cause.

of court the foremost state affair: it logically leads to systematic demoralization. And all the evils spring from a common root. The underlying principle of the *l'état c'est moi* maxim is applied also to the court—of course apart from its relation to the king: no duties, only rights. Here is the essential difference between the absolutism of the *ancien régime* and that of Prussia under Frederick William and Frederick the Great: they made—not only by the profession of their lips, but in fact—their duties the basis of their rights: " The King is the first servant of the state." Louis XIV. had adopted for himself, and, consequently, also for his court, the opposite principle, and the result is thus summed up by d'Argenson: " The court! all the evil is in this word. The court has become the senate of the nation; the last lackey of Versailles is senator; the chambermaids have a share in the government, if not to order, at least to prevent laws and rules; and, thanks to their preventing, there are no longer either laws, orders, or rulers. . . . The court is the tomb of the nation."

Of course! Even when under Louis XIV. frivolity reached its climax, these people were not satisfied with eating, drinking, and dressing well and amusing themselves, they also hungered and thirsted for power, as well for its own sake, as for the sake of all that power is able to procure. The means by which power was sought and obtained necessarily were in accord with the spirit bred by the maxim: No duties, only rights. To a degree, and with certain very important restrictions, merit was a good thing, but the art to ingratiate oneself was better still. Statecraft was not proscribed, but skilful intriguing—and in that lackeys and chambermaids could lend a most helpful hand—was often a much surer road to power; and to hold one's ground for any length of time without being more or less of an expert in this low craft was next to impossible. Was it under such circumstances not inevitable that the welfare of the country should often consciously be relegated to the position of a secondary consideration, and still much oftener, in questions not of capital import, not be taken into consideration at all, simply because it never occurred to one that it might be proper to do so?[1]

[1] On the 11th of May, 1777, Joseph II. wrote from Paris to his brother Leopold: "Un despotisme aristocrate y (à la cour à Versailles) règne ; cela paraît contradictoire et cela est pourtant vrai. Chacun dans son département y est maître absolu, mais avec la crainte continuelle d'être, non dirigé

This is a most important point. Most of these men and women were far from being so wicked as one might infer from what I have said thus far. They would be judged very unfairly, if one did not more or less apply to them the Saviour's prayer on the cross: Forgive them, for they know not what they do. The court was the tomb of the nation, but it was as well a charming as a brilliant tomb. The courtiers were wonderful masters in the art of making it a fairly bewitching abode, and they thoroughly enjoyed inhabiting it. It was, however, not only a fact, that they principally lived for enjoyment, but, for aught they knew,

par le souverain, mais déplacé. Par-là chacun ne tend qu'à se conserver, et aucun bien ne se fait que s'il est analogue à cette vue. Ceux qui ont voulu faire autrement, en ont été le sacrifice et renvoyés sur le champ. Le Roi n'est maître absolu que pour passer d'un esclavage dans un autre. Il peut changer des ministres, mais il ne peut jamais, s'il n'a un génie transcendant, se rendre maître de la gestion de ses affaires.

"Vous pouvez-vous imaginer comment les affaires se traitent. Pour moi, je vois manifestement que toutes les petites qui ont trait aux intrigues personnelles, se traitent avec le plus grand soin et intérêt, pendant que les majeures, qui regardent l'état, sont parfaitement négligées. Toute la robe et la noblesse, qui a pour but de parvenir un jour à une place de ministre, crie continuellement contre ceux en place pour qu'on les change, mais quand on voudrait attaquer cette forme détestable du despotisme affreux que chacun exerce dans sa charge, tous se réunissent pour l'empêcher, chacun espérant a son tour y parvenir."—Arneth: Maria Theresia und Joseph II., 133.

it was also their indisputable right to make enjoyment the chief aim and end of life. Those were, perhaps, not far from right, who afterwards said, that fully to know what a refined pleasure life can be made to be, one must have lived in those days. Yes, refined to the last degree of exquisiteness. However hollow or even rotten the inside, the form was of masterful design and the polish unsurpassable in lustre and delicacy. Coarseness of any kind sends an unfeigned shudder to the very bones. Even "the great goddess Lubricity," to use Matthew Arnold's graphic metaphor, is worshipped without hypocrisy, but in a tasty drapery purloined from Chastity's wardrobe. In every respect the senses are allowed more than their right, but whatever is grossly sensuous is of decidedly bad taste, and whatever is of bad taste is a social sin harder to be forgiven than many a serious moral failing. The true perfection in form does not only become "a second nature," but it supplants nature. Even Mirabeau, whose last brief illness was accompanied by excruciating pains and most cruel torments, smilingly asked his friend La Marck: "Well, *Monsieur le connaisseur* in beautiful deaths, are you satisfied?"[1]

[1] Mém., VIII. 478.

How then can it surprise one that to the real adepts of the art of living of the *ancien régime* it is afterwards much easier to mount the scaffold with an easy grace above criticism, than to overcome their repulsion against using the uncouth means of defence, with which they alone could have defended themselves successfully?

But here is the rub: the perfection of form supplanted nature. The pleasures of the intellect and even of the soul were appreciated as much, and frequently more than the mere pleasures of the senses, but Essence was always the page having to carry the train of the mistress Form. When to make a proper bow had become a science, it is easy to understand that there was a strong tendency to let talking degenerate into turning fine phrases, to think that the tickling sensation produced by a new idea dispenses one from the duty of earnestly inquiring into its truth, to mistake sentimentalism for sentiment, to substitute social etiquette for morality.

There is something stern in truth of every kind —the very idea of truth implies sternness. Sternness, however, is incompatible with perfect enjoyment, as the term is understood by the society of the *ancien régime*. Therefore, enjoyment being its chief aim and end, it is not really truthful in anything—in its feeling and thought just as little as in its action. It plays a part with itself and, in consequence, over-acts its part. It is sufficiently tired of pleasure in the usual acceptation of the word to be eagerly in quest for sentiment—food for the soul—and it literally pins its sentiments to its dresses and sticks them into its coiffures. "Enthusiasm," as Taine says,[1] "was obligatory." But a gentleman characterized this enthusiasm by the following caustic remark: "A true sentiment is so very rare a thing that, when I return from Versailles, I sometimes stop in the streets to look at a dog gnawing a bone."[2]

---

[1] I. 210.
[2] Champford 110.—Quoted by Taine, I. 204. Emperor Joseph II. wrote (May 11, 1777) from Paris, to his brother Leopold: "Il y a des objets à voir très-intéressants, des établissements dont l'appareil et l'apparence est superbe, l'on bâtit avec une recherche et un luxe étonnant, enfin l'on met tout à l'apparence, mais quand on va plus loin et qu'on recherche vraiment l'utile, on est très-détrompé. Ce n'est pas celui-là qui est une jouissance froide, peu saillante et par conséquent peu accueillie par cette nation vive et légère, qu'on cherche pour faire parler de soi, car c'est là à quoi tend tout le monde ici ; on veut avoir l'apparence des grands sentiments qui ne sont point encore des vertus, et l'on se contente d'acquérir de la célébrité par-là, ne fût-ce même que pour huit jours. A cet objet l'on sacrifie tout, et l'on ne connaît guère dans cette Babylone, ni les lois de la nature,

Satiety of over-refinement has so far set in, that it longs for some new stimulating spice, and, under the guidance of Rousseau, it finds it in nature, never suspecting that it is a hazardous undertaking to play at nature in gold-embroidered coats and on mirror-like floors: heretofore the children had been abandoned to the servants, now the inspiration received from the new gospel went with some ladies to the extent, that they deemed it fit to do their maternal duty by their babies in the salon in the presence of gentlemen. As to the actualities of life the *l'état c'est moi* principle was under Louis XVI. of as good service to the court as under Louis XIV.; but as the fathers and grandfathers had already been born with it into the world, it no longer offered any charm to either the intellect or the imagination. To these the new political philosophy ministered the keenest relish, and why not indulge them also? In the royal theatre of Versailles the whole court enthusiastically applauds the verses from Voltaire's "Brutus":

> " *Je suis fils de Brutus et je porte en mon cœur*
> *La liberté gravée et les rois en horreurs.*"

Why not?

ni celles de la société, que pour un certain vernis de politesse."—Arneth : Maria Theresia und Joseph II., II. 132, 133.

Ah, why not! Under the *ancien régime* France existed for the court, but did nothing but the court exist in France? Were there not people to whom what these verses expressed might be already now, or might become in a not-distant future, something more than a fine abstract sentiment and a good text for an animating political discussion, without any reference to the real world? Or was, perhaps, the court after all prepared to applaud also a serious attempt to have this sentiment with all its logical consequences carried out in practice? Even if there had been one man or woman ready to bring all the personal sacrifices this implied, even his or her heart would as yet have been chilled with horror at the idea of the black treason against the king it also implied. Many thought that they fully and honestly believed in the doctrines of the new political philosophy, and in a way they really did. There was only one little difficulty about it: they —if the homely saying may be excused—wanted to eat the cake and yet keep it. They did not only pin their sentiments to their dresses and stick them into their coiffures, they also practiced them, but without really and wholly giving up— either in theory or in practice—their old notion that it is for the *grand seigneur* to say, when and how far the rights of common mortals ought to be respected by him. They did ardently long to exchange the after all rather wearying artificiality of their studied conventionalities for the freshness and unconstraint of nature, but nature was of course to stalk on high-heeled shoes, to wear stays, and to stitch lace cuffs to the coat sleeves. They were honest votaries of liberty, and did look forward with delight to a state and society constructed according to the dictates of enlightened reason, but—to paraphrase a legal term—with the benefit of their privilege-inventory of the *ancien régime*. In a word: they were victims of the strange illusion that they could aspire to the new and at the same time hold fast to the old. Ségur writes: "Liberty, whatever its language might be, pleased us for its courage; equality, because it was so convenient. One enjoys descending, as long as one believes one is able to mount again as soon as one pleases; without forecast we enjoyed at the same time the advantages of aristocracy and the sweets of a plebeian philosophy."

The same writer says: "The institutions remained monarchical, but the customs became republican." It would have been more correct to write: the thinking and feeling, and, consequently, in a measure, even the customs became republican. But when the thinking and feeling, and therefore also the customs of the people are no more in accord with the institutions, these are merely empty shells. The only questions are, when and how they will be crushed. Posterity can clearly see, that in this case the answer to both these questions was not doubtful. Louis XIV. had departed this life, burdened with the hatred of the people; on Louis XV. rested, long before his death, the unmeasured contempt of the whole nation. The contempt of the people is, however, an infinitely heavier and more fatal burden on the shoulders of a monarch than their hatred. And, if the contempt for the person of the monarch is coupled with the hatred of the institutions, the burden becomes crushing. Now when the character of the institutions is eminently monarchical and the putrefaction that is eating up the monarchical summit, has not only seized upon all the political institutions, but has also made much headway in the decomposition of the whole social structure, the break-down must be complete and ensue with a terrible crash.

LECTURE III.

Mending the Old Garment with New Cloth.

LOUIS XV. proved himself not only a monstrous cynic, but also a keen observer and sound reasoner, when he uttered that word, which would alone secure unenviable immortality to his memory, " *Après nous le déluge!* "[1] He risked nothing in leering with contemptuous unconcern at the lowering clouds, but when he died it was proposed to bestow upon his young heir the surname " *le désiré,*" the longed-for. By sheer force of habit the loyal attachment to the Bourbons was still so strong that the successor of Louis XIV. " *le Roi-Soleil,*" could defile the purple to any ex-

---

[1] The phrase is perhaps more correctly attributed to Mme. Pompadour, if, indeed, either of them is the author of it. But though it be apocryphal, it characterizes Louis XV.'s way of feeling, thinking and acting as correctly as the *L'Etat c'est moi* that of Louis XIV. The other phrase attributed to him : *Cela durera autant que nous*, is probably more authentic, and it amounts to pretty much the same thing.

tent without having to fear that he would be called to account by the people; and he was too sagacious to let his government become guilty of any inconsistencies in the sins of omission and commission, which systematically fostered the rotting of state and society. But he had filled the vessel of the people's forbearance so to the brim, that his successor was greeted with eloquent silence on his first visit to the capital, merely because he had not as yet commenced the cleansing of the Augean stables by forthwith dismissing the two best hated ministers, Maupeou and Terray; and he was alive to the necessity of reforms, but only just enough to make bad worse. However rotten a house may be, it stands astonishingly long, if it be but left to itself. In a certain stage of decay, its power of resistance is increased by its being equally rotten in all its parts. Finally, it must fall in any case, but the catastrophe is hastened on by tearing down a part here and there and rebuilding it with new and sound material. The rotten rest is not capable of sustaining the weight of the new pieces. Just because the new is sound, it causes the old to break down sooner than it otherwise would have done. Thousands of years ago it was known that it may be foolish to mend an old garment with new cloth. This Louis XVI. undertook to do, and if ever there was a man possessed of all the qualities required for making the worst of such an unpromising undertaking, it was he.

His father had not allowed him to grow up in the poisoned atmosphere of the court. That, however, was about all he had done for him, and that was a scanty outfit for the absolute ruler of a great empire drifting at an alarming rate into all-embracing political and social decomposition. But little effort had been made to make up by thorough training in some measure for the deficiencies in nature's ungenerous endowment. His intellectual horizon was narrow, and even within its compass he moved but slowly, and no more than he could help. Indolent, and yet irascible; good-natured, and yet curt to rudeness; yielding to every pressure, but allowing no one to gain full sway over his ever-vacillating will; rendered stubborn by the very consciousness of his weakness, and sinking back into redoubled weakness as soon as the fitful mood of asserting a will of his own has spent its force; in spite of his weakness, standing before an insurmountable barrier whenever his religious belief is or seems to be involved in the question at issue, but even then not stirred up into striking a vigorous blow for his convictions, but only intensifying into absolute immovability the listless passivity, which is the very essence of his nature; well-meaning, but devoid of the intellectual as well as of the moral strength required to persist, when his good intentions meet with resistance; morally pure, but without any adequate conception of either the nature or extent of moral responsibility.[1]

And just in this, the most essential quality, the queen was even more wanting, though in every other respect greatly his superior. Later on, when the revolutionary storm had burst in full force from the clouds, Mirabeau called Marie Antoinette, in a momentary access of enthusiastic hopefulness, "the only man at court." She had unquestionably a much stronger will and more

[1] La Marck, as true a friend as the hapless royal couple ever had, thus sums up his opinion in a letter of Oct. 10, 1791, to Mercy d'Argenteau: "Louis XVI. est incapable de régner,—par l'apathie de son caractère,—par cette rare résignation qu'il prend pour du courage et qui le rend presque insensible au danger de sa position,—et, enfin, par cette répugnance invincible pour le travail de la pensée, qui lui fait détourner toute conversation, toute réflexion sur la situation dangereuse dans laquelle sa bonté a plongé lui et son royaume."—Corresp. entre Mirabeau et La Marck, III. 248.

initiative as well as a keener intellect than her royal husband, and therefore her ascendency over him grew apace with the increasing troubles and dangers. But the reason that to the last he never implicitly followed even her lead is not to be sought exclusively in his character. Though in the scorching heat of her trials she intellectually and morally matured almost beyond what one could have expected of her, she remained to the end intellectually and morally utterly unable to lay down for herself a clearly-conceived course, or to pursue her course with unswerving steadiness and determination. Apart from her attitude in her trial and on the scaffold, she never rose to being really great in a great time, but always betrayed the illy-balanced woman, who cannot refrain from allowing petty considerations of every imaginable kind to interfere more or less with the decision of capital questions. And what was ultimately lack of the required elevation of judgment, purpose, and fate-defying energy, had been originally shallowness, fickleness, and frivolous unconcern. Louis understood from the beginning that his inherited vocation of kingship not only conferred rights, but also imposed duties, and however dim his ideas of them were, he did not shirk them, though his sluggish mind derived no real satisfaction from their performance, and his locksmith-workshop was much more attractive to him than the cabinet council. Marie Antoinette thought the life-task of a queen consisted in enjoying herself and helping her friends to have a good time of it. Only so far as it was serviceable to these ends did she at first try to exercise an influence on questions of state, and all attempts to kindle in her a sustained interest in any other serious occupation proved sad failures.[1] All the charges that have been laid to

[1] Among the sincere devotees of the old order of things, perhaps none has a better claim to be considered a classical witness as to the character of the queen than Besenval. He writes: "La reine est loin de manquer d'esprit, mais son éducation a été nulle sous le rapport de l'instruction. Hors quelques romans, elle n'a jamais ouvert un livre, et ne cherche pas même les notionséque la société peut donner; dès qu'une matière prend une couleur sérieuse, l'ennui se montre sur son visage et glace l'entretien. Sa conversation est décousue, sautillante et voltige d'objets en objets. Sans aucun fonds de gaieté personnelle, elle s'amusait de l'historiette du jour, de petites libertées gazées avec adresse, et surtout de la médisance comme on la prépare à la cour; voilà ce qui lui plaît. Facile, point exigeante, mais peu faite pour le sentiment.... Dans le temps que la confiance qu'elle me témoignait m'avait autorisé et excité à lui donner des conseils, j'ai tout fait pour l'engager à acquérir des connaissances qui l'eussent mise à portée de se livrer à la prétention qu'elle avait de faire des ministres, et de déterminer ou détruire une décision d'administration; mais je ne pus obtenir qu'elle mît un peu d'application à la place des frivolités qui remplissaient le vide de ses journées.

her door, with a view to make her appear wicked, are malicious distortions or wholly unfounded slanders. She was only thoughtless and frivolous; but her thoughtlessness was of a kind to provoke malice and slander,[1] even if she had been surrounded by saints, instead of the putrescent court inherited from Louis XV. and Madame Dubarry; and her frivolities went to such excesses, that under the existing condition of things, they could not but have the effect of crimes against the commonwealth. That in all she did and left undone she did not swim against the stream, but only allowed herself to be gayly carried along by it, goes far toward mitigating the moral judgment that has to be passed upon her, but it could be of no avail as to the consequences.

Does it require uncommon discernment to see that the hapless fate of this royal couple—he hardly out of his teens, she still in them, and both

[1] "C'est avec ce manque de moyens que l'archevêque de Sens la fit entrer dans tous les comités, et lui donna une voie prépondérante dans les décisions. Par ce moyen, il augmentait son crédit, la reine n'étant que l'écho de son opinion; mais cette conduite ne pouvait manquer de donner un tort à cette princesse, et de jeter un ridicule sur elle, en même temps qu'elle discréditait l'administration."—Mémoires, II. 309, 310. Compare the letter of Joseph II. to his brother Leopold, May 11, 1777.—Arneth, Maria Theresia und Joseph II., II. 134.

so moulded by nature that even fifteen years later they are still but overgrown children—was irrevocably written in that surname, "*le désiré*," which paints the whole appalling situation so drastically in one word? A man of a different stamp would have derived from it not only inspiration, but also strength; Louis XVI. was chained down by it to the task of working from the first days of his reign systematically at his own doom. His heart readily responded to the nation's pressing call for reform, but he utterly failed to realize, that as to the outcome of the promptings of his heart, everything depended on what his head stood for in the question. Not officially prime minister, but virtually the head of the cabinet, was Maurepas, a cynical and wily old courtier, whose principal merit consisted in having been exiled in punishment for a biting lampoon on Mme. Pompadour, the late king's mistress, who had long been the virtual sovereign of France. To embark on the stormy sea of reform with such a man at the helm was certainly a venturesome undertaking. Nothing would be more erroneous than to infer from this choice, which was imposed upon the weak monarch by his aunts,[1] that the king was not perfectly

[1] The king had resolved to make the former minister,

honest in his desire to fulfill the just expectations of the people. It was manifestly only an error of judgment, but of such grossness, that even chance would be powerless to keep the craft

Machault, prime minister, but the imperious princess Adelaïde induced him by her importunities to change the address of the letter. Mme. Campan writes : " La lettre pour appeler M. de Machault était écrite, lorsque madame Adelaïde obtint la préférence de ce choix important en faveur de M. de Maurepas. On rappela le page qui était muni de la première lettre." And she adds in a foot-note : " Ce fait a été mis en doute ; mais je puis assurer que Louis XVI. s'adressa à M. de Campan pour rappeler le page ; qu'il le trouva prêt à monter à cheval, le fit remonter pour rendre sa lettre au roi lui-même ; et que la reine dit à ce sujet à mon beau-père : ' Si la lettre eût été parti, M. de Machault eût été premier ministre ; car jamais le roi n'eût pris sur lui d'écrire une seconde lettre contraire à sa première volonté." —Mém. de Mme de Campan, I. 88. The letter itself bears witness to the truth of the story. It would surely not have contained certain expressions if it had been originally intended for Maurepas. Besides Mercy, who was unquestionably well informed, directly asserts that Maurepas owed his appointment to the aunts of the king. He writes on May 17, 1774, to the empress : " Le premier soin de Mesdames a été de se mêler de matières de gouvernement, de donner des conseils, de proposer qu'on fît venir le comte de Maurepas, et la reine, de complaisance en complaisance, a servi elle-même d'organe pour faire parvenir au roi les idées de Mesdames, ou pour mieux dire, celles des intrigantes qui les dirigent."—Arneth et Geffroi, Marie-Antoinette, Corresp. secrète entre Marie-Thérèse et le comte de Mercy-Argenteau, II. 146, 147. This *début* is eminently characteristic of Louis XVI.

out of the currents running with irresistible force straight on to the breakers.

Still at first the prospects were apparently bright enough. Turgot, the *contrôleur général*, assisted by Malesherbes, launched the reform vessel with such vigor in the right direction, that under the animating effect of the applause and gratitude of the people even Louis was momentarily stirred up into something like zest and zeal. Turgot proved that the credit of the government was by no means irretrievably ruined, and that, with the restored credit of the government as a starting-point, the sanitation not only of the state finances, but also of the whole economic life of the nation, could be successfully put under way. To free the government from its financial embarrassment, however, meant the sealing up of the one source from which any immediate political dangers were to be apprehended; and if but a direct political contest with the people was obviated, progressing economic sanitation could be made to furnish a basis of sufficient extent and solidity to bring about gradually the required political, social, and moral regeneration. Only one thing was in the nature of the case utterly impossible : not even the first steps towards the sanitation either of the state finances or the nation's economic life could be taken without violently jostling against those who had a selfish interest in the maintenance of the existing vicious system, and these embraced all who possessed power or could exercise influence. Not every reform hurt them all, but by every step forward some wasp's nest was stirred up, and soon all who fattened upon the follies or vices of the *ancien régime* were tacitly leagued against the audacious minister, for they were quick to learn that they were bound up in a common cause.

The most effective weapon had been furnished to the opposition by Maurepas. Despite his cynicism he relished popularity, and as Maupeou's dismissal had been so vividly applauded, the undoing of what had rendered him so hateful to the people—the suppression of the Parliament—was sure to be hailed with still greater exultation. So it was, but it also started ill-boding reflections as to the nerve this government was likely to display, whenever it had to encounter popular clamor. "What you want to be considered an amnesty," warned Turgot, "will be deemed an *amende honorable* and a confession of weakness;[1]

[1] He saw even then that weakness constituted the

therefore the Parliament will prove bolder and more intractable than ever, while you expect from it meekness and gratitude. You enter upon the arduous work of reform by restoring to its enemies their most formidable stronghold, for with the Parliament revives its right to register the royal edicts, and it is sure to refuse the registration of one and all that strike a blow against the interests of the privileged classes." [1]

Louis followed Maurepas' advice,[2] but when

greatest danger for the success of Louis XVI.'s reign, and with the experiences of every month this conviction grew upon him. His letter of April 30, 1776, to the king contains the oft-quoted solemn warning : " Do not forget, Sire, that it was weakness which put the head of Charles I. on the block ; it was weakness which formed the League under Henry III., which made crowned slaves of Louis XIII. and of the present king of Portugal ; it was weakness which caused all the misfortunes of the late reign." This most remarkable letter has been published in full by Larcy, Louis XVI. et Turgot, 27-31, and it deserves to be carefully read from the first to the last word. Turgot has erected himself by it a *monumentum œre perennius.*

[1] The import of the restoration of the Parliament is pointedly summed up by Rocquain in the sentence : " Le monarque détruisait l'ouvrage de Louis XV., et donnait raison à la nation contre la royauté."—L'Esprit révolutionnaire avant la Révolution, p. 323.

[2] The Journal historique, VI. 301, Nov. 8, 1774, reports : "Sur les diverses représentations faites au Roi concernant le danger pour son autorité de rétablir le Parlement, S. M. a répondu : cela peut être vrai, c'est peut-être mal vu en

the course of events proved how good a prophet Turgot had been, he let himself be persuaded to compel the registration of two incisive reform edicts—the abolishment of the road service (*corvée*) and of the guilds. It was a worse than barren victory for the good cause. On the 12th of March, 1776, the "bed of justice" had been held, and exactly two months later Turgot was dismissed. He was only a high-minded patriot and a great statesman, and things had come to such a pass, that these qualities could not suffice to maintain a minister in his post. It is no exaggeration to say that they were, on the contrary, disqualifications, which rendered his speedy fall inevitable. The approval or disapproval of the people at large was as yet wholly irrelevant as to this question; and as Turgot had necessarily hurt, offended, or at least alarmed, all whose approval or disapproval was not irrelevant, his only support was the king, and, though legally everything depended exclusively on him, his approval was actually under such circumstances quite as irrelevant as that of the people at large. More than

politique, mais il m'a paru que c'était le vœu le plus général, et je veux être aimé."—Quoted by Oncken, Das Zeitalter Friedrichs des Grossen, II. 571, 572. Also this is eminently characteristic of Louis XVI.

eleven years later Jefferson wrote, without any qualification as to circumstances: "The king goes for nothing."[1] "Only Turgot and I love the people," Louis plaintively said, and yet he consented to dismiss him, though he had pledged his word of honor unswervingly to sustain him. According to his conception of his political duties, a sigh sufficiently atoned for his straying from the right path.[2]

Marie Antoinette did not even sigh. She had contributed to Turgot's overthrow in petty anger over his having caused the recall of a certain diplomat whom she was pleased to honor with her good opinion. It was her first unpardonable political sin.

If a fair judgment is to be passed upon her folly and the king's weakness, one must, however, not leave out of sight that even many of those who could derive only benefit from Turgot's reforms, rejoiced in their unreason at his removal, and that

[1] 8th of Oct., 1787, to Jay.—Works, II. 294.
[2] It is, however, not to be denied that the critical notes of the king to Turgot's memoir on the "*Municipalités*" go far towards justifying Professor Oncken's opinion, that Louis' confidence in the soundness of Turgot's policy was severely shaken.—See Soulavie, Mém. historiques et politiques, III. 147-154.

also those who regretted it the most were exceedingly far from understanding its full import. In regard to just the most essential point they seem hardly to have seen much clearer than those who were in high glee. Their victory could not have been more complete than it was, for there were not only to be no more reforms, but even what Turgot had achieved was not allowed to stand: Clugny, his successor, forthwith repealed the edicts abolishing the road-service and the guilds. One thing, however, neither Clugny nor any power on earth could undo: the fact that the reform-ministry had existed, and that its history had made certain impressions upon the thought and feeling of the people, could not be blotted out, and this fact was a living, working, originating force. And Turgot's adversaries applied themselves to the task of making it such with an energy and ingenuity, which must recall to one's mind that saying of the ancients, "Those whom the gods wish to destroy they first make mad."

Turgot had stripped the shackles of internal duties from the grain commerce within the empire, and thereby removed the main cause of that astounding fact, that more or less of famine in some part or other was rather the rule in this country so blessed by nature. In acknowledgment of the inestimable boon, the so-called flour-war was waged against him, the real originators and organizers of which had to be sought up to the very footstool of the throne. It never occurred to these high-born gentlemen that the lesson they now taught the mob might not be obliterated from its memory as soon as it suited them. Ah, if the mob had a genius for anything, it was the art of purposeful bread-riots. Systematized holding up of the transports, especially those destined for Paris, destroying rather than plundering them, insisting upon having the price arbitrarily fixed by the government, without regard to the market value, placards threatening to hang the minister and even the king himself[1] —it remembered everything so well fifteen and sixteen years later, that it could perform the terrible comedy to perfection unbidden and unassisted by its quondam teachers, and even greatly improve upon them. This chapter of the history of the

---

[1] Rocquain, p. 330, gives the following samples of placards : " Louis XVI. sera sacré le 11 juin et massacré le 12 "; " Si le pain ne diminue pas, nous exterminerons le Roi et tout le sang des Bourbons "; " Si le pain ne diminue pas et si le ministère n'est pas changé, nous mettrons le feu aux quatre coins du château."—Mirabeau's uncle, the *bailli*, wrote : " Si je ne me trompe, de pareilles émeutes ont toujours précedé les révolutions."

reform-ministry certainly went far towards making the complete victory over it an earnest of ultimate crushing defeat.

And another lesson the masses had learned from it quite unaided was still infinitely more potent in this respect. When Clugny re-established the *corvée*, open force had to be used to get the peasants to work again at the roads. Could a more ingenious way have been found to embitter the people than to make them fully conscious of the weight of their burdens by taking them off for a little while? And, in consequence of his being dismissed, Turgot had worked altogether only to this end—the embittering of the people. Because he had not been allowed to do *more*, all *that* he had done served only to shake the masses from their lethargy into consciousness of the unbearableness of the existing order of things. And when they had been made to feel their just grievances more keenly by a partial redressal of the same, hopelessness was added to bitterness. Hopelessness—for at the bidding of all the cormorants feeding upon their vitals, Turgot was ignominiously kicked out *because* he had dared and proved himself able to do for all France what he had done as intendant for poor Limousin; and, to cap the climax, a well-meaning king, who had appointed him for this very reason and purpose, did it despite himself. Could there after this still be anything for them to hope from the government? And what did a negative answer to this question signify to a people so systematically educated to letting the government do all the thinking, willing, and acting for it? Turgot's overthrow did not tempt the masses to rise in revolution. Its effect—I do not venture to say upon their thinking, for as yet they hardly did any as to these questions, but upon their feeling—was a much more dangerous one. A ray of light had flitted before their eyes, and now their outlook into the future was again the old leaden blank, only its oppressive dulness several shades darker than ever before. The consequence was that, unless other agencies brought about a revolution, the doom of France was irrevocably sealed, for what progressive paralysis is to the individual, the listlessness of hopelessness is to a nation. On the other hand, however, if a revolution were brought about by other agencies, it would indeed inevitably become a deluge, for the masses would necessarily be hurled from one extreme into the other, because everything had concurred to keep their political instincts in the embryonic state, and the madness of their unreasoning enthusiasm might prove to be even more terrible than the fury of their unbridled resentment. To save France without a revolution by reform had been rendered impossible by Turgot's overthrow.

That the government would make fresh attempts at reform, was not only possible, but more than likely. Its financial distress would compel it to do so. But if it had become impossible to save France without a revolution by reform, reform, while it might defer a revolution, must evidently render its ultimate outbreak more certain.

Necker, to whom the department of finances was confided, when, a few months later, death happily put an end to the most disreputable administration of Clugny, was thoroughly convinced that his taking the reins was in itself salvation assured. That his successes apparently justified this overweening self-confidence was the greatest misfortune. He was not a statesman, but only a good financier, and even that not in the higher sense of the word. Only in all the resources and artifices of the craft of banking was he really great, and these qualities ultimately worked as a curse, because they were with him not the complement of, but the deceptive substitute for, genuine statesmanship. They made him utterly mistake the true nature of his task. In his eyes it was confined to procuring the necessary means for keeping the machine in motion. The brilliant manner in which he managed to do that, not only confirmed his self-deception beyond the possibility of ever being disabused, but also deceived the people more and more about his abilities and the character of his achievements. Public opinion not only met him half-way, but pushed him vigorously on in the wrong track he had taken, because his banker's skill found the principal field of its application in procuring the funds required for the prosecution of the American war. That he did not realize the tremendous political effects this war was to have upon France, cannot be laid especially to his charge, because he was only as blind as all the rest. But he, above all others, was bound to foresee its disastrous financial consequences, and they rendered it his solemn duty to warn his colleagues and the king against embarking in this venture as earnestly as Colbert had warned Louvois and Louis XIV.[1]

---

[1] Turgot had done so in March, 1776, and for the moment not in vain. He deprecated the idea of engaging in such a war as the greatest calamity, "because it would render im-

He, however, did exactly the contrary. He prided himself on being able to procure the money, and he did so all the more, because he procured it without increasing the taxes. And for this very reason the people enthusiastically cheered him as an incomparable miracle-worker. Mirabeau's eye pierced through the dazzling halo to the rotten core. He wrote: "What you account his glory is his crime. . . . Credulous people! Make haste to admire him; some day your children will curse him." To get even with England for the disasters of the colonial war, the rulers of France, lustily applauded by the people, made the present eat up what belonged to the future, and thereby pushed her over the brink of the precipice.

The indirect effects of the way in which Necker contrived to meet the government's financial needs fully equalled in perniciousness the direct results. His financial operations scattered broadcast the germs of a virulent speculative fever. Stock-jobbing, with a chronic bull tendency, became a wide-spread craze and fast degenerated into unprincipled gambling at the expense of the unsophis-

possible for a long time, and perhaps forever, a reform imperatively demanded by the welfare of the state."—See Daire, II. 571.

ticated but covetous public. The epidemic, sedulously fostered by Calonne's system, raged far into the revolution, and contributed greatly towards plunging it into its maddest excesses. Mirabeau's father prophesied in 1785, when Necker was no longer in office: "I tell you point-blank, that the imminent crash will be brought about by Necker's system, and if I had a better stomach, I should expect to see it yet as I have seen that of Law." [1]

While thus the qualities from which Necker mainly derived his strength as a financier, in the end wrought but sad havoc, he also did really good work by introducing order, method, and honesty into the administration of the finances, suppressing many useless offices, curtailing the profits of the tax-farmers, and so forth. But though these reforms were by no means so paltry as has often been asserted, they could do nothing towards averting a catastrophe. On the contrary, they even helped to make it more certain, by provoking resentment here, and deepening the delusions there, as to the worth of his state-craft.

In both respects his celebrated *compte rendu* was still infinitely more effective. The publication of this report on the administration of the finances

[1] Loménie, III. 682.

and their actual condition was undoubtedly Necker's most momentous political deed; but it is a very different question how far it can be justly accounted a great merit. Not to enhance the merit unduly, one must above all not fail to notice a most important fact: the publication was, in a measure, made under compulsion. The credit of the government had by this time become so strained that it could no longer be maintained without giving the creditors of the state some information about the situation. This cause of the bold step, together with Necker's boundless vanity, determined the character of the report. It was very far from presenting a true picture. More than anything else most scrupulous truthfulness was needed, and the minister palmed off upon the country a deliberate falsehood. Yes, though it did not contain a single incorrect item, it was a gigantic falsehood; not however, as Haeusser thinks, owing to dexterously deceptive grouping, but principally in consequence of what it did *not* contain. By the simple stratagem of ignoring one-half of his subject he figured out a surplus of ten millions for the ensuing year, while the full accounts resulted in a deficit of almost 219 millions. Sooner or later the bold juggler would be found out, and when the truth became known, direful consequences were a matter of course. From the political point of view, however, the most essential thing was the fact in itself that he had said anything at all, no matter whether what he had said was the truth or not. It was an unprecedented proceeding, for absolute secrecy was one of the most characteristic traits of the administration of the *ancien régime*.[1] The people were denied any right to know, think,[2] judge, or will in regard to it. Now the government confessed by its act that it was constrained to let them know, and that was the virtual acknowledgment of their right to think and to judge, while it conceded nothing as to a right to will. It was an appeal to public opinion, but without summoning it to cooperate in an organized legal way, an invitation to criticise without subjecting it to the restraint of

---

[1] In 1775 Malesherbes, at the time President of the *cour des aides*, had submitted to the king a memoir urging that the *clandestinité* pervading the whole tax system be done away with. Turgot recommended the publication of the Memoir, but Maurepas prevented it. Malesherbes had even ventured to write : " Personne ne doit vous laisser ignorer que le vœu unanime de la nation est d'obtenir ou des états généraux ou au moins des états provinciaux."

[2] It is eminently characteristic that one of the gravest charges brought by the court against Turgot was his prefixing explanatory introductions to the royal edicts. To give the people reasons, it was said, is to degrade the crown.

the responsibility imposed by the right and duty to act, a lusty application of whip and spurs, but the bridle kept carefully stowed away in the saddle-bag.

It is safe to say that history knows of no other financial report that has had an equal sensational success. Even on the ladies' toilets the *compte rendu* lay next to the scent-bottle. The courtiers, however, were maddened by the way in which he had exposed them in their quality of bloated parasites. Goaded by their attacks his vanity betrayed him into furnishing himself the petard with which he was hoisted.

To find a suitable successor was less easy than it had been to get rid of him. For two years one got along somehow with Joly de Fleury and d'Ormesson, letting time, wind, and weather go on doing their work of destruction upon the old garment. They did it so effectively that one could no longer close one's eyes to the necessity to put the helm once more into the hands of a man professing to have something really deserving the name of a financial policy. Calonne offered himself, the courtiers found him admirably suited to their wishes, and a clumsy intrigue sufficed to impose him (October, 1783) upon the king, although the first suggestion had aroused his indignation, because Calonne had the reputation of being a paragon of bold frivolity and profligacy. The charge was more than borne out by his *début*. He requested the king to deliver him from the importunities of his creditors, brazenly intimating that in case of refusal he would know how to obtain the money by means of his new office. Louis knew the argument to be irrefutable. He went straight to his desk and took out 230,000*l*. in stocks—10,000*l*. more than the minister had asked. The scene is equally characteristic of both men.

Calonne did not propose to sew patches of new cloth on the old coat. He was going to renovate it, as the dealers in second-hand clothing renovate the cast-off garments of the rich. A finer piece of work of this kind was never turned out. The old coat not only looked sleek and trim, but shone with dazzling brilliancy. As to how it would wear—ah, well, chemicals that produce such wonderful effects are apt to be rather hard upon the fibre.

Calonne's maxim was: If you are in distress for money don't noise it about, but spend lavishly. The public, believing that you have much, will readily lend you all you want. It worked excellently.

The king was more than reconciled to his brilliant minister, and the courtiers were in the seventh heaven of delight. One of them said: "I knew well that Calonne would save the state, but I did not expect that he would do it in the twinkling of an eye." The miracle-working maxim was, however, no new invention. From time immemorial it was the main article in the catechism of every bankrupt swindler, and therefore the dashing minister had to end as every swindling bankrupt ends. Loan followed loan in rapid succession, but the spending went on at such a rate, that when a new loan was contracted, its proceeds were already squandered. After three years the game was up. The Parliament could no more be induced to register and the capitalists buttoned their pockets.

It was not pleasant to drop from the sublime flight into the cold water of stern reality, but Calonne was nothing daunted. As it was swim or drown, swim he would. As there was no other choice, the saving of the state had after all to be done by the prosaic and wearisome process of reforming. He went at it with all the frivolity he had displayed in laying down and carrying out his first programme. I do not mean to say that his propositions were frivolous. He had charged Dupont de Nemours, Turgot's most prominent disciple, with the drawing up of the plan, and it was therefore in the main only a revised edition of Turgot's reform programme. But if it be doubtful whether this programme would have sufficed at that time, it is most certain that it was now sorely insufficient. And what of it, if that had not been so? Was it not the acme of folly to suppose that *he* would be able to put through a programme which had dragged a Turgot down when the government was still in the actual possession of the plenitude of its powers, and that *he* would be able to accomplish this after the infinitely more modest demands of a little order and economy had overthrown a Necker?[1] Reforms, exacting considerable sacrifices from powerful classes, cannot be effected by a man who is justly considered the very incarnation of frivolity. For certain political tasks a character challenging a high degree of moral respect is an absolutely indispensable requisite: an infinitely more critical

---

[1] Mirabeau wrote, on the 24th of March, 1787 : "La réputation de l'homme est le plus grand obstacle à la chose." —Lettres à Mauvillon, 201. For brevity's sake I shall thus quote the "Lettres du comte de Mirabeau à un de ces amis en Allemagne."

juncture, the revolution, furnished an infinitely more portentous illustration of this all-important truth.

As the Parliament was sure to offer a most determined opposition, Calonne induced the king to have the reform-propositions submitted to an assembly of Notables. I am not prepared to assert that the historical lumber-room of France contained instruments better adapted to his purposes, but this was surely egregiously unfit. It was a representative assembly, and yet in no sense did it really represent the people; it was composed exclusively of members of the privileged classes, even the few that were to figure as representatives of the third estate, *i. e.*, of the overwhelming majority of the people, being of the privileged minority of their own order, and all the members were not elected, but appointed by the king.

The Notables did exactly what one had to expect from such a body. The reforms proposed by the minister cut deepest into the flesh of the clergy, and it was principally the clergy that unhorsed him. Mirabeau wrote: "It is much less to the public cause than to the clergy that the Notables have sacrificed Calonne." [1]

[1] Loménie, IV. 88.

It is, however, more than questionable whether Calonne had been guilty of indulging in any delusions about what might be expected, either from the high-minded patriotic liberality or from the political sagacity of the Notables, which ought to have told them that the refusal to give something might eventually lead to having all taken. His idea had been, in fact, to submit neither the Whether nor the How to their decision. Before they met the edicts were all ready and printed for promulgation, *i. e.*, the Notables were simply to say "Aye, aye," to whatever the government wanted. To induce them to do so, he relied upon his glib tongue, court influences, and all sorts of stratagems, as the dividing of the assembly into seven bureaus, each presided over by a prince of the royal family. What would the achievement have amounted to if his expectations had been realized? The Notables had no legal authority whatever; the value of their consent consisted only in its moral weight.[1] But

[1] In the Memoir in which he proposed to have recourse to the expedient of such an assembly as Henry IV. had in 1596 (Soulavie, Mém. historiques et politiques, VI. 120–132), Calonne himself emphasized, that only from its being backed by public opinion could one expect to attain the intended results. Such an assembly he declared, " est le seul moyen de prévenir toute résistance parlementaire, d'en imposer aux réclamations du clergé, et de forcer tellement l'opinion

could *such* a consent of an assembly *thus* constituted and *thus* composed be expected to have much moral weight with the nation? One fine morning the following placard adorned the fences of Paris and even the minister's own door: " The new theatrical company organized by M. de Calonne, which is to commence its representations on the 29th of this month, will play as the principal piece, *The False Confidences,* and as a by-play, *The Forced Consent;* these plays will be followed by an allegorical pantomimic ballet, entitled *The Cask of the Danaides.*" Did not the author of these biting sarcasms betray sounder political judgment than those who with Thomas Jefferson expected great things from this assembly, although the Notables refused to perform the " Forced Consent," and, in consequence, the ballet, called " The Cask of the Danaides," could, as a matter of course, not be danced? The establishment of provincial assemblies after the pattern of those organized by Necker (1778) as an experiment in Berry and Haute-Guyenne was the only reform worth mentioning to which the assembly consented.[1] Jefferson, there-

publique, qu'aucun intérêt particulier n'ose élever la voix contre le témoignage prépondérant de l'intérêt général.

[1] Cassagnac says very correctly: " Les Notables n'avaient

fore, was surely on the wrong track when he wrote:
"The king, who means so well, should be encouraged to repeat these assemblies."[1] The king, however, had been still infinitely farther off the right way, when he wrote to Calonne the day after the convocation of the Notables had been resolved upon: "I have not slept this night, but from joy." The courtier came nearer the truth, who dryly remarked, "The king resigns." And he came nearer the truth, because Mirabeau was right when he wrote from Berlin to Talleyrand, "I deem the day one of the brightest of my life, on which you apprise me of the convocation of the Notables, which undoubtedly will precede by but little that of the National Assembly.[2]"

That is the decisive fact. Jefferson did not over, but grossly underestimate the import of the convocation of the Notables. It was, however, the fact of their being convened that in itself rendered it an event of world-wide import, and the import was doubled just because, in the nature of things,

aplani aucune ancienne difficulté et ils en avaient levé cent nouvelles."—Hist. des Causes de la Révolution, II, 137.

[1] Febr. 28, 1787, to Lafayette. Jefferson's Works, II. 131.
[2] Loménie, IV. 89. Mirabeau (Mémoires, IV. 339, 340) claimed to have suggested to Calonne the convocation of the Notables. Assuming the assertion to be well-founded, the advice has to be judged in the light of this declaration.

the hopes set upon them had to prove cruel delusions. The convocation of the Notables was an onward move in the direction into which the government had been launched by Necker's *compte rendu*, and it was the *decisive* step forward.[1] It was the confession, that the government felt unable to cope any longer single-handed with its difficulties and was compelled to ask the co-operation of the nation by representatives. The *l'état c'est moi*, the claim that immutable divine law condemned the people to be nothing but an *object*, was virtually abandoned. Though it was not intended to concede anything whatever as to the question of *right*, they were actually acknowledged to partake also of the nature of *subject*, i. e.,

---

[1] The speech of the keeper of the seals, Lamoignon, at the close of the Assembly, contained the following remarkable sentence: "Vous avez été le conseil de votre roi; vous avez préparé et facilité la révolution la plus désirable, sans autre autorité que celle de la confiance qui est la première de toutes les puissances dans le gouvernement des Etats." (Wéber, Mémoires, I. 177). The government was getting into a way of using the word revolution, which is striking and very suggestive. So far from feeling any concern about it, one becomes anxious to improve every opportunity offered to fructify the growing fascination it exercises upon public opinion. It does not occur to these wise gentlemen that a word readily turns into a live force, and that even in a lantern a burning candle is a dangerous plaything, if one be seated in a pile of dry straw.

dire necessity had now wrung from the reluctant government for public opinion also the right *to will*. Having in fact yielded the principle, no power on earth could prevent its legitimate and logical consequences being forced upon the government. To play off the Notables as the legitimate organ of public opinion, *i. e.*, the nation, was a mockery, and to propose the limiting of their task to serving the government as a speaking-trumpet was a fraud. Therefore, on the one hand, the government could not possibly derive from them the benefit it expected; and, on the other, as it had acted under the irresistible compulsion of its situation in calling them, the failure rendered impossible effectual resistance to the demand of summoning to its assistance a genuine representation of public opinion with a formal *bona fide* acknowledgment of its right to a co-determining will. The Notables, with whom Calonne undertook to mend the old garment, were, in a sense, not a piece of new cloth. He unearthed it from the tomb of the past, where it had lain for more than a century and a half. The patch was so decayed, that it tore in the attempt to mend it on. And the very dust and mould of the grave that lay on it, rendered it so heavy, that under its weight the garment itself was rent in twain from end to end.

Brienne, Calonne's successor, had no difficulty whatever in ridding himself of the Notables, who had served him as a footstool to climb into the minister's chair. They were, indeed, glad enough to go, when, after the overthrow of Calonne, they could no longer screen their obtuse selfishness behind virtuous declamations againt the criminal frivolity of the *contrôleur général*. Nothing, however, could be mended by sending them home. The mischief was done, and it was irretrievable. That Brienne did not at once submit to the inevitable, but had once more recourse to the Parliament to help the government out of the lurch, only rendered bad worse. The Notables had been convened, because the ears of the Parliament were irrevocably closed against Calonne. No one possessed of the slightest knowledge of the history of the contest between the government and the Parliament could, however, indulge in the delusion, that the main cause of the latter's intractability was the obnoxious personality of the minister. By the turn things had now taken, this personal element went for nothing in the question. Unless the gentlemen of the Parliament were as blind as bats, they could not help seeing that they were compelled to appear more than ever to be in dead earnest in their alleged determination no longer to hold the candle for the government and brook its governmental methods. The all-pervading and all-embracing despotic paternalism had logically resulted in rendering opposition to the government *in itself* highly meritorious in the eyes of the people. To this most portentous disposition of public opinion, the Parliament owed its intoxicating popularity. It completely veiled the eyes of the people to the fact that the Parliament, being the apex of a privileged class, in truth contended, like the other privileged classes, for the maintenance of its own power and its own prerogatives,[1] while it ostensibly carried the ban-

[1] Mirabeau wrote, Oct. 4, 1788, to his father: "Ces aristocrates à robe noire, ces insatiables privilégiés qui veulent dépouiller le roi, mais uniquement pour se doter de ses dépouilles."—Mém., V. 196. Even Louis XVI. fully realized that. As early as 1776 he wrote: "My Parliaments have been in the habit of yielding everything that is demanded of them, when it bears only upon the people at large. They are in the habit of refusing everything, and of submitting to hardship and exile, when any revenue is required to their individual detriment." He added: "Were I to call together the landholders of my kingdom, and to require them to assess themselves, this would be the very way to excite them to oppose the revenue demanded. Abbé Terray clearly found, that one is never sure

ner of popular rights and fought for the people's interest. There were appallingly few who understood Mirabeau, when he wrote: "For ten months I am the target of all imaginable calumnies, because I do not share the parliamentary fanaticism, and have not written a line in favor of this opposition. I always was of opinion, that there is between king and Parliament another small party, called the nation, to which all sensible and honest men should belong."[1] To allow itself to be outdone by the Notables and palpably to lag behind them, meant nothing less for the Parliament than to drop from its face the deceptive mask as to the

of carrying a tax into effect, unless it is to be imposed by the party that pays no part of it, or that pays a very small part of it."—Soulavie, Hist. and Polit. Memoirs of the Reign of Louis XVI. Translated from the French. III. 147, 148. I have several times quoted the original of the work from notes taken in former years. Here I have been unable to procure the original, but in the Boston Athenæum I found this English translation.

[1] Aug. 21, 1788. Lettres à Mauvillon, 374. On the other hand, however, he bluntly refused to comply with the solicitations of the minister Montmorin to enter the lists for the government against the Parliament. "Je ne ferais jamais la guerre aux parlemens qu'en présence de la nation," i. e., in the States-General. (Mém., IV. 480.) So long as these were not convened there was, in his opinion, only the choice between two evils, and by far the smaller of the two was the selfish and impure opposition of the Parliament: "que la volonté seule du roi fait la loi" he deemed infinitely worse.

true character of its opposition, and to turn the enthusiastic applause of the people into contemptuous wrath. The Notables, however, had refused to serve the government as a crutch, and some of the members of the Assembly had dared to pronounce with most impressive emphasis the great word, which of late had been heard more than once, the States-General. New negotiations between the government and the Parliament were indeed not thereby precluded, and if all the legitimate and illegitimate means of persuasion still at the disposal of the government were dexterously brought into play, it was even still possible that once more a way would be found to tide over the decision by a nefarious bargain at the expense of the suffering people. But it was utterly impossible to prevent a new clashing of the two powers for any length of time, and as soon as they clashed no choice was left to the Parliament.

It is true, to put an end to the tediousness of its exile at Troyes it did consent to another bargain, and it would not be easy to hunt up a more ignominious one in all the records of history.[1]

---

[1] In vain d'Esprémenil, the leader of the opposition, exclaimed with hot indignation: "We have left Paris covered with glory, and we shall return to it covered with dirt."

But it soon became aware, that it had thereby driven the first nail into its own coffin. The quarrel at once broke out afresh, and the Parliament no longer shrunk from fully accepting the situation created for it by the Notables. It did not stop at entering a formal protest, when the government proceeded to peremptorily impose obedience by a *séance royale*, a modified form of that death-bed of legal resistance, misnamed "bed of justice." It anticipated the intended *coup d'état* of the government by a unanimously-adopted declaration purporting to set forth the unalterable fundamental laws of the realm. This declaration cast the government with tied hands and feet into the roaring sea of its financial embarrassments, for according to it one of these unalterable fundamental laws was the right of the people to vote the taxes by the regularly-convened and regularly-constituted States-General.[1] And no brute force

[1] It is deserving of notice what the king had written in regard to regularly convened States-General, when in 1776 Turgot in his curious and most remarkable Memoir on the "Municipalités," suggested the creation of a kind of permanent popular representation. "The idea of giving existence to perpetual States-General is subversive of the monarchy, which is only absolute, because its authority does not admit of a partner. The instant such an assembly shall have commenced, there will no longer be any intermediate agency

was to avail it in any attempt to cut the fetters. It was beforehand branded as legally null and void, and in case the Parliament were broken down by the strong hand, the principles laid down in the declaration were to stand committed to the care and protection of the king, the royal family, the peers, the estates constituting the nation, whether assembled or not assembled, collectively and individually.—That was a terrible thrust home, directed with fatal precision against the most vital point of the *ancien régime*; yes, not only against the supreme political authority of the *ancien règime*, the government, as the Parliament believed and intended, but against the *ancien régime* itself, and the Parliament was an integral organic part of this *ancien régime*.

Apparently the Parliament was completely worsted. From the government's point of view

between the king and the nation, but that of an army; and it is a horrible and painful extremity to entrust to an army the defending the authority of the state against the assembly of the French people. The system of M. Turgot is a beautiful vision—it is the utopia of an individual, projected by a man who has excellent views, but which would overturn the present state of France. The ideas of M. Turgot are extremely dangerous, and ought to alarm us by their novelty."—Soulavie : Hist. and Polit. Memoirs of the Reign of Louis XVI. Translated from the French. III. 148.

the *coup d'état* was now no longer only morally and politically justified, the declaration had rendered it an imperative necessity. Forcible resistance to the decree of the 8th of May, 1788, abolishing the old magistracy—a *cour plénière* supplanting the Parliament of Paris, and new superior courts, called *grands baillages*, the provincial Parliaments—was out of the question. One of the greatest and most essential institutions of the *ancien régime*, and that very one which was upon the whole unquestionably the soundest, or rather the least rotten, successfully crushed and entombed by the supreme government of the *ancien régime*—that was the singular achievement of the Brienne cabinet, if one did not look beyond the day. Looking into a not distant future, the character of the momentous victory was more correctly described by an advertisement pasted on the palace of the late Parliament and reading thus: "Palace to be sold, ministers to be hung, crown to be disposed of."

The Parliament of Toulouse had replied to the *coup d'état* of the 8th of May by declaring: "There being no longer any barrier between the king and the people, nothing is left to the latter but the consciousness of its strength." That was not so. There was no lack of champions for the seemingly lost cause. In some parts of the realm the representative bodies entered the lists to tilt a lance against the government. At least for the purposes of opposition the vitality of the old provincial estates now proved to be by no means extinct: and the new provincial assemblies, the establishment of which might have done a great deal towards averting a catastrophe, if it had been attempted twenty or thirty years earlier, had in the main only stimulated the process of general disintegration, because resorted to at the eleventh hour.[1] In several provinces the nobility boldly pushed to the forefront, leading the van in the fray, with reckless unconcern as to the eventual ultimate consequences to itself, even not scrupling to stir up the masses. Nobility and Parliament were equally blind as to the true nature of the game they were engaged in. And the clergy, as I

---

[1] Besides, the sound idea underlying the reform was carried out in a most bungling way. The administrative powers conferred upon the provincial estates to a great extent virtually dismounted the old administrative apparatus, without, however, substituting another for it. Nor was this the only reason why the reform necessarily had to result in systematically anarchizing the country. See as to this most important question, Tocqueville, L'ancien Régime et la Révolution, b. 3, c. 7.

shall point out in my next lecture, did not see a whit clearer, though the method of its suicidal onslaughts upon the *ancien régime* was mostly a different one—I should fain say the opposite. The oddest and most significant feature of the political wrangles leading to the revolution is that it was by the beneficiaries of the *ancien régime*, the privileged orders, that the government was driven from pillar to post, and finally forced to capitulate.[1]

As to practical importance, this feature has, however, to contend for the honor of the first place with another, to the closer observer apparent enough throughout the struggle, but now in the last decisive hour glaring forth with such intensity, that everything else is almost swallowed up by its lurid effulgence. Not the strength of the assailants carried the day. This government,

---

[1] "Qui avait accoutumé le peuple aux atroupemens et à la resistance? les parlemens. Qui, dans les provinces, avait montré le plus d'hostilité contre l'autorité royale? la Noblesse. Qui avait refusé avec le plus d'opiniâtreté de venir au secours du trésor, et employé le plus d'astuce pour se soustraire aux charges publiques? le Clergé. Ainsi c'étaient véritablement les parlemens, la Noblesse et le Clergé qui avaient seuls déclaré la guerre au gouvernement, et donné le signal de l'insurrection; le peuple n'était là que comme auxiliaire."—M. de Lameth: Histoire de l'Assemblée Constituante, I. 100.

which had arrogated to itself the exclusive right to think, will, and act for the nation, suddenly stood exposed before the people and the whole world in the total impotence of abject senility. Nobody heeded the behests of its intendants, its judges were desecrated and hooted at, its very sabres stuck fast to their scabbards or had lost their edge. Its claim to be the state had been made good by it for more than a century, so far as it was within human possibility to do so, and now of a sudden the whole governmental machinery came to a dead stop. The government had not been overthrown, for nobody had attempted or even wanted to do that; it lay prostrate, because it had not had the strength to keep on its feet.

Did that only mean, that the dismissal of Brienne had become a matter of course? Clearly not. Immense as was the popularity of Necker, who succeeded him, it would have melted away faster than freshly-fallen snow in the April sun, if he had presumed to act as if nothing had happened. Though his boundless vanity forbade him to doubt that the state was saved, by the fact in itself of his being recalled to the helm, he understood, or at least instinctively felt, that at least as to one thing, Brienne had at last read the signs of the times correctly: the days were past when the government could exercise any volition as to the calling of the States-General.[1] Brienne's blunders had not been the cause of, but only furnished the occasion for, the stoppage of all the wheels. Therefore a lever had to be applied to the mechanism to put it again into motion, and this was the only one that had not yet been tried; all the others had proved to be so rotten, that they had broken into splinters in the attempt to keep it agoing. Whether this one would stand the test, nobody could tell. Thus much, however, was certain, that it was cut out of wood of an essentially different fibre. But while for the present only conjectures were possible as to the positive side of the experiment, its portentous negative side stood revealed in terrible clearness. This—to use once more my first metaphor—was not merely another

---

[1] Mirabeau had not only foreseen but also foretold the government that it must inevitably come to that. He had written to Montmorin as early as Apr. 18, 1788 : " Ne voyez-vous pas que les états généraux sont aussi nécessaires comme la seule ressource des finances que comme moyen unique de constituer le royaume, et *vice versa ?* qu'en un mot il n'y a de difficultés dans tout ceci que celle que l'on se suscite à soi-même, ou qui résultent de cette terrible maladie des ministres, de ne pouvoir jamais se résoudre à donner aujourd'-hui ce qui leur sera infailliblement arraché demain."—Mém., IV. 483.

effort to make the old garment hold together by patching it up with a piece of new cloth. Though the political obtuseness of king, court, and minister was much too dense, consciously and fully to abandon this impossible project, the government, by summoning the States-General to its aid, in fact formally and officially declared, not indeed *royalty*, but the *ancien régime*, bankrupt—completely and irretrievably—not only in the literal, but in every sense.

LECTURE IV.

The Revolution before the Revolution.

THE convocation of the States-General, I said at the close of my last lecture, was the formal official declaration that the *ancien régime* was bankrupt—completely and irretrievably—not only in the literal, but in every sense. To-day I have to show that what the government by the convocation of the States-General admitted to be a fact —that, and even more than that—had been a fact for a long time. It had not only become an impossibility to maintain any longer the political system of the *ancien régime*, but as a political and social system it was dead a long while. But its legal interment had been deferred. This the government had been able to do, because state and society, though of an organic nature, differ in this from the individual organism, that they also partake of the character of a machine.[1] Though

---

[1] The fundamental mistake of the political metaphysicians consisted in deeming admissible and even necessary to con-

the vital forces be completely spent, machine-like they are kept in motion by the impetus originally imparted by these. Unless a catastrophe be precipitated by outside pressure, they may thus go on for generations and even centuries. But if the governmental machinery is allowed to get so out of gear that all the wheels only clog each other, the whole fabric must instantly commence falling to pieces. On the other hand, it is in itself proof absolute that a political system and social order must have been dead a long time, if upon the breaking down of the governmental machinery the whole fabric instantly goes to pieces, as the spoils from the graves crumble into dust when exposed to the air.

The institutions of a country derive their vital energy exclusively from the feeling and thinking of its people. The more they get into discrepancy with these, the more they become impediments of life, instead of being its regulators and incentives. In France, however, the feeling and thinking of the people had become more and more

---

sider and treat them as nothing but a machine. Siéyès bluntly asserted: " Jamais on ne comprendra le mécanisme social si l'on ne prend pas le parti d'analyser une societé comme une machine ordinaire."—Qu'est-ce que le tiers état ? 75.

not only estranged, but consciously opposed to the institutions of the *ancien régime*. From different quarters systematic and most persistent attacks had been directed against them with ever-increasing effect. And, though the assailants were prompted by different motives, wielded different weapons, and brought their battering-rams to bear against different points, in a sense, all the charges ran upon convergent lines: the intersecting point was the general principle underlying all the institutions, the very spirit of the *ancien régime*. It, therefore, would have been strange indeed, if ere long a methodical siege had not been consciously laid to this very spirit. Only when this was commenced, it became fully apparent how successful the preceding attacks upon its different concrete manifestations had been. While these had all had as determined adversaries as champions, it is but little exaggeration to say that this last onset was hailed by all. Their reasons for doing so considerably differed, and none of them realized the full import of their acclamations, but the gratification they felt proved that—whether they were themselves aware of it or not—the *ancien régime* had no longer any living roots, either in their hearts or in their minds.

We must pursue the history of this process more in detail. By this preliminary characterization of it, however, one fact is clearly revealed—the most important one of all. The primary cause of the death of the *ancien régime* was not inanition. *Purposely* root after root was *cut*, until none were left to convey any sap to the trunk. In other words, though the *ancien régime* underwent a process of mummification, the nation had not lost its vitality. It grandly manifests itself in the vast intellectual labor, the principal aim and end of which is the cutting of those roots; but these efforts absorb its energy to the almost total exclusion of everything else. "Louis XIV.," says Lemontey, "asked France for a single publicist, and she did not answer him." With every decade this held good more and more in regard to everything. France could still boast of great minds, but their services were no more at the command of the *ancien régime*; they were the leaders of the different opposition hosts.

It was the government's doing. Narrow-mindedness had caused it to declare relentless war against the principle of progressiveness, the force of habit and the indolent unconcern of cynicism kept it from turning back into the right way, and to be helped out of momentary difficulties of one kind or another, it allowed itself from time to time to be pushed on in the wrong direction by those who were too engrossed by their selfish interests to perceive, that by too much zeal in their pursuit they worked with equal effectiveness at the government's and their own ruin.

If it is asked, who did the most towards the destruction of the *ancien régime*, the correct answer is, beyond all question, Louis XIV., its greatest representative. In every respect he inoculated the germs of death into the system, and by extending the *l'état c'est moi* principle over the spiritual domain, he laid the axe to its very roots. By setting himself up as lord-absolute over the consciences of his subjects, he forced the current of historical evolution to run backward, for the principle, not indeed of religious liberty, but of its precursor, religious tolerance, had already obtained legal recognition in France. It had worked beneficently, and no political necessity or even expediency could be alleged as a reason for breaking it down. The revocation of the Edict of Nantes did not only strike a hard blow at the material prosperity of France, by causing the expatriation of vast numbers of her most industrious and skilful citizens, of even more consequence was the debilitating effect it had upon the Catholic Church of France by depriving it of the stimulus of friction with differing, though kindred, ideas. Toleration of friction is, however, incompatible with the *l'état c'est moi* principle. As there is of right but one will, also but one way of thinking is admissible. Louis XIV. was only consistent when he did within the Catholic Church of France what he had deemed his right and his duty to do in regard to the Huguenots. But the effect was not the same. To smother Jansenism, and to compel obedience to the *constitution* of the bull *Unigenitus*, which the Holy See (Clement XI.) issued at the instigation of the king's father-confessor, the Jesuit Le Tellier, was to close the safety-valve while stoking the fire under the boiler. There was no use in crying ever louder and more imperiously: Down! The harder the serpent *Opposition* was knocked on the head, the deeper it inserted its fangs. If it had only, or but principally, been a question of creed, it might have been different, for the times were past when all the higher interests and aspirations of men were focused in their religious opinions. But it soon became in the main a political contest, and the political contest was of such a nature that the opposition, in casting its eyes about for effective weapons, was compelled more and more to press forward towards fundamental principles and to apply them to all the relations of human life.

An alliance—defensive and *offensive*—with ultramontanism, that was the true purport of that climax of Louis XIV.'s warfare against Jansenism, his accepting the championship of the bull *Unigenitus*. Therefore he and his successors, so far as they trod in his footsteps, had to encounter henceforth the resistance, not only of the Jansenists proper, but of all who thought the liberties of the Gallican Church and the spirit breathing in them a possession worth fighting for. To coax or force the recalcitrant members of the clergy into submission was by no means to terminate the contest victoriously. Rather the contrary. Oil was poured on the glowing coals, for ultramontanism grew the more exacting, the less there was of open dissent among the prelates. As late as 1775, Turgot's and Malesherbes' exertions in behalf of the Huguenots, demanding for them again the right of worship or, at least, that of concluding legal marriages, was met by the bishops by presenting in person a written protest to Louis XVI., insisting upon inexorable execution of all the harsh laws passed since the revocation of the Edict of Nantes and the completion of the suppression of Protestantism. And the government was ever ready to work the bellows by acceding to the demands—trampling under foot not only individuals, but also the Parliaments —whenever, for pecuniary or political reasons, it stood in need of the church authorities. But it also almost as readily turned against them, if what it deemed its paramount interests for the time being invited it to do so: fanning the flames as a rule from the right side did not prevent its fanning them occasionally also from the left. The suppression of the Jesuits in 1762 by no means completely and definitively severed the alliance between the crown and ultramontanism, but it nevertheless was a tremendous blow struck for the opposition. It was not, as Rocquain says, "the first breach in the edifice of the *ancien régime*,"[1] but it was the first breach in it made by the law. As to public opinion—if one has the

[1] "Aux yeux des contemporains, l'abolition de la Société de Jésus ne fut pas seulement la destruction d'un institut détesté, mais l'ébranlement de tout un ordre de chose qui pesait sur la France depuis le commencement du siècle. Ce fut une première conquête de l'esprit révolutionnaire, une première brèche opérée dans cet édifice de l'ancien regime qui apparaissait fondé sur l'alliance du despotisme royal et de

educated classes in view—there was no longer any need of making breaches in regard to ultramontanism; orthodoxy, nay, even Christianity, had already been battered down to a fearful extent. This work of destruction was continued with such effect, that since **1785** the General Assembly of the clergy refrained from publishing any "*Actes*," by which it had been wont to exhort the people to remain true to the faith, and suppressed the pensions which it had paid to clergymen of literary ability for "writing up" the faith and the cause of the church. It tacitly confessed its utter defeat and abandoned the field. Henceforth when this highest representative body of the French church appears on the scene, it is no more as the representative of religion, but only as that of a privileged class. In this character, however, it remained to the last true to its past. When, in 1788, Brienne requested its support against the Parliament for his tax-edicts, it replied by emphatically asserting the old claim, that the church could not be subjected to any direct tax;[1] but at

l'ultramontanisme."—L'Esprit révolutionnaire avant la Révolution, 233.

[1] Remontrances du clergé, présentées au roi, le dimanche juin 1788, sur les droits, franchises et immunités du clergé.—Archives Parlementaires, I. 377–384.

the same time it declared, that "the French people is not taxable at discretion," and endorsed the demand of the Parliament, to have the States-General convened.[1] To shield its own interests, says Rocquain, "it called the revolution." Church and crown in looking at the outcome of the alliance of 1713 might well quarrel as to which of the two had got, not indeed the best, but the worst of the bargain.

Church and crown were the vanquished; but who were the victors? Not the Jansenists. Long since the pennons had been grasped by other hands that spurned the shield. They did not defend; to attack was their creed. In other respects they differed not a little among each other, using different weapons, and, consequently, also different tactics. This tenet, common to all of them, was, however, of such paramount importance, that they rightly considered themselves a close fraternity,

[1] "Le peuple français n'est donc pas imposable à volonté. La propriété est un droit fondamental et sacré; et cette vérité se trouve dans nos annales, quand même elle ne serait pas dans la justice et dans la nature. . . .

"Depuis les premiers Etats généraux jusqu'à ceux d'Orléans et de Blois, le principe ne se perd jamais de vue, que nulle imposition ne peut se lever sans *assembler les trois états, et sans que les gens desdits états n'y consentent*."—Remontrances du clergé, présentées au roi le 15 juin 1788. Archives Parlémentaires, I. 375.

calling itself *the philosophers*. Ultramontane historians never tire of bringing the accusation against the Reformation, that it begot the so-called philosophy of enlightenment of the 18th century. In a sense the charge is not without foundation. Without the former, the latter could never have come into existence. But there is this cardinal difference between the reformers of the 16th and the *philosophers* of the 18th century, that the former wanted to reform the church, while the latter devoted all their energies to writing it down.[1] In this they were most powerfully aided by the wondrous advances of the sciences. Inherited beliefs were so hard pressed by the onset of demonstrated facts, that reason, which had heretofore never been allowed an equal chance when coming into collision with dogma, found itself, on a sudden, fighting from strong vantage-ground. If science could not be refuted by simply pointing to the catechism, why then should the church have a right to dispense itself from answering the questions of reason? The implicit submission to authority was shaken to such a degree by science,

---

[1] Voltaire's *écrasez l'infame* is in truth the motto of all, though they do not all choose quite unreservedly to declare it to the public, or even to confess it to themselves.

that the inalienable right of reason to institute a never-ending cross-examination as to the claim of being an absolute authority, or, for that matter, any authority at all, was readily admitted. Men were eagerly—though not always over-earnestly—in quest of truth, and soon came to brand as incompatible with the dignity of man the accepting of anything as truth on the strength of alleged unchallengeable authority from on high. Whether truth can really be elicited *only* from science and reason, or whether an irrepressible craving of the human mind does not peremptorily demand the assumption of a third source, which must at least be permitted to serve as a complement of the other two, though the claim to control and overrule them be disallowed—this decisive question was disposed of with flippant levity or wholly ignored. But even mocking laughter and cutting taunts were allowed to pass for victorious arguments. Reason was not only reinstated in its right, but put on the altar. Yes, not merely the throne, but the altar. Not only obedience was rendered, but worship offered and exacted. The conquering fraternity never became fully consolidated into a party, but the hotter the fight waxed, the more it was wrought into a sect by the glow of passion.

Voltaire repeatedly speaks of "our Church." But he also complains, that the "brethren" lay themselves open to the charge of speaking, like their adversaries, too apodictically.[1] How could it be otherwise! Having substituted another absolute and unchallengeable authority for the one they tried to overthrow, they necessarily drifted into dogmatism in fighting it. Just as necessarily they also became as intolerant as their adversaries, for intolerance is not the offspring of any particular kind of dogmatism, but whoever says dogmatism also says intolerance.

That the warfare of the philosophers took this deplorable turn, was partly due to their other handmaid, the so-called classicism, which pervaded the whole intellectual life of the educated classes to such an extent, that we find it far into the revolution exercising a most portentous sway over the minds of nearly all the leading men. Its dominant traits were an almost conscious aversion to the particular, definite, and concrete, with a corresponding excessive fondness for the general, vague, and abstract, and a mania for systematizing. Although science lifted the philosophers into the saddle, observation was with them only the groom of logic

[1] VIII. 148.

and abstraction. The consequence was, that the charger Reason took the bit between the teeth, madly rushing off into the quagmire of system-craze.

That was the more dangerous, because the disciples, as is their wont, soon outran the masters. Public opinion, created and made a power by the philosophers, grew fast to be even less tolerant than they.[1] It became an inappealable law unto itself. That something was the prevailing opinion came to be considered as in itself sufficient proof of its being true. Therefore, to contend against public opinion was to contend against truth, and to contend against truth was to be a self-confessed fool or knave. Thus the worship of reason logically led to bidding reason step back and take the second place. Not that public opinion claimed the right to set aside and overrule a verdict of reason; but by assuming its decisions to be always, as a matter of course, in conformity to reason, it actually erected itself into the court of last resort. Men thought they had fully emancipated

[1] Necker wrote in 1784: "Most strangers find it difficult to form a conception of the authority which public opinion exercises to-day in France; they comprehend with difficulty what this invisible power is, which commands even in the palace of the king."

themselves, and in fact most of them had to a fearful extent only changed masters. Nothing could be further from the truth than to suppose that the vigor and daring with which public opinion strikes at the inherited authorities, furnishes the right measure of the intellectual and moral courage of the individuals. They stand in an inverse ratio to each other. The noble aspiration to mould public opinion is rapidly supplanted by eagerness to swim with it. Thereby it is more and more rendered a yoke. By the time it is elevated to the position of a legal authority its rule has become so confirmed, that it needs only to have the opportunity offered to turn into a more ruthless despotism than that of the worst Bourbons. And it is to encounter no barrier, either in its own doctrines or in the political instincts of the masses, for there is one tenet in the creed of the *ancien régime* the philosophers left untouched: they not only did not shake, but even greatly strengthened, the direful belief in the omnipotence of legislation.

This points to a fact of the utmost importance. The philosophers were first and above all not the fathers, but genuine children of their time, and because they were that, they exercised such a tremendous influence upon it. It is strange that even many historians of eminence have failed fully to understand this. The French literature of the 18th century has often been called the main cause of the revolution. That I do not put a low estimate upon it as a factor in the historical evolution issuing in the revolution, has certainly been made sufficiently apparent by what I have said already. But I nevertheless assert, that a literature never has been, and never will or can be, the primary cause of a revolution, because in the nature of things it is always itself primarily a symptom. To satisfy oneself that this is the case here also, it suffices to notice, that ere under the influence of the writings of the philosophers, vaguely floating tendencies have taken definite shape as conscious public opinion, other agencies are at work in the same direction with equal energy and as much effect. At the middle of the century this stage had not yet been reached, as the publication-dates of most of the more important works in question conclusively prove. Yet d'Argenson writes at that time: "The exiled gentlemen of the Parliament ... have begun to study the public law in its sources and discuss it as in the academies. In the public mind, and from their studies, the opinion is being established, that the nation is above the King as the church is above the Pope."[1] And those lines throw a flood of light on the true situation not only on account of the time when they were penned. Even after the philosophers have—without slackening their attacks upon the church—entered with full force upon their war against the existing political system, they argue the question, what the public law *ought* to be. Here we find the magistracy of this early date discussing the question, what the public law *is*. Nor was this discussion ever again to stop. Under the impressions of the disasters of the Seven Years' and the Colonial War, the contentions between the government and the Parliaments are not only revived with great acerbity, but they assume besides an essentially different character. The crown is compelled to argue its claim to absolute power and tries to prove its legality; and, on the other hand, the Parliaments set up the claim to be, in the aggregate, a representation of the nation, and as such at least a co-ordinate, if not a superior power to the crown.[2] Voltaire wrote in December,

---

[1] Taine, I. 385.

[2] In 1763, the Parliament of Paris proclaimed the doctrine, that to impart the force of law to the royal edicts they must

1760: "Gentlemen of the Parliament will soon burn the edicts of the Lord King."[1] From this may be inferred the degree of spiritedness with which the magistracy conducted the discussion. As to its effect upon the public, we may form an opinion by what d'Argenson had written the year before: "A philosophical wind of free anti-monarchical government is blowing; that enters into the minds. . . . Perhaps the revolution would meet with less resistance than one thinks; it might be effected by acclamation."[2] When the government finally put its heel upon the Parliaments, it was too late. The ideas and catchwords had sufficiently taken root in all classes of the people to work as self-active forces.

Also in the warfare against the church the Parliaments played an independent and important part. Though they had officially to contend against the philosophic spirit, the magistracy, like the other educated classes, became thoroughly im-

---

be registered by all the thirteen Parliaments. In the same year that of Rouen—"non comme Parlement particulier de Rouen, mais comme classe du Parlement général séant à Rouen"—demanded that an account be published of the revenues and the expenses of the state.

[1] Corresp. gén., VII. 221.
[2] Taine, I. 385.

10

bued with it. We are told, that it was no uncommon thing to let the hangman throw some waste paper into the fire instead of the books that had been condemned to be publicly burned: these were brought to the judges as a highly prized addition to their private libraries. That is a most genuine trait of the *ancien régime*: the public authorities lustily making grimaces at themselves. But the Parliaments being what they were, it was quite as much a matter of course with the magistrates, that their private opinions about the teachings of the philosophers were not to interfere with upholding all their rights as public authorities and as the representatives of a privileged class. When Turgot and Malesherbes undertook to apply those teachings, the Parliaments at once made common cause with the church authorities, with whom they had been thrown into a protracted and bitter contest by the bull *Unigenitus*. On the other hand, however, they had struck in this contest many a telling blow for those rights, and the effect of those blows could not be confined to what they had been intended to accomplish. While Voltaire pretended to think it possible that the Parliament might eventually go to the extremity of burning royal edicts, the Parliament of Aix in 1765 actually condemned a brief of Pope Clement XIII. to be burned by the hangman. After such exploits there was no use in again concluding an alliance with the church. Though prompted by different motives and proceeding in a different way, the Parliament had as effectively as the philosophers sawed off the roots, with which the church of the *ancien régime* was imbedded in the heads and in the hearts of the people, and this work of destruction could no more be undone by such an alliance, than a rootless tree can be kept alive by gluing roots to the trunk.

From still a third quarter the existing order of things was simultaneously assailed with vigor and systematically. It is true, the economists are comprised in the philosophers, if the designation is understood in its broader acceptation. In the main, however, they form a distinct group, though the leading economists also try their hands in the field that is more especially tilled by the philosophers proper, and some of the leading philosophers also dabble in economics. Voltaire's article on grain (*blé*) in the *Dictionnaire Philosophique* is considered by some to mark an epoch in the history of the war upon the political system, while Turgot as early as 1757 preached the revolutionary doctrine, that the individuals have rights which the commonwealth may not infringe, because they, the individuals, exist independently of it, but that the corporate bodies (*corps particuliers*—perhaps orders would render the meaning more correctly) within the commonwealth must cease to exist, when they cease to be useful, for they have been created by and for the commonwealth.[1] The economists were also a sect, "political philosophers," as Bachaumont (III. 318) calls them, "destined to overthrow all the accepted principles in regard to government and to build up a new order of things." Lack of time compels me to refrain from entering upon this chapter of the history of the revolution before the revolution. I can add but one word to what I have incidentally mentioned about it in my last lecture. The reform ministry now presents itself in a new light. With Turgot and Malesherbes "the philosophical spirit" was formally admitted into the government and for a while even allowed to take its supreme direction. We can now realize the full import of this fact, for we now know that "the philosophical spirit" was, so to speak, but another name for deadly enmity to the *ancien régime*.

[1] Article "Fondation" in the Encyclopædie, VII. 75, § 6.

After the economists had had their day, the "patriots" stepped into their place. As is already indicated by their name, politics in the stricter sense of the word was their special field. "Going back"—as the continuator of Bachaumont says—"to the origin of laws and the formation of governments, they have pointed out the reciprocal obligations of subjects and sovereigns, and fixed the great principles of administration."[1] The result of their disquisitions can be summed up in the following sentence from one of their writings: "There are people on the earth, who of right can call the sovereign to account for his conduct."[2]

Surely, in itself a result of no small moment. But to make clear its whole portent, attention must be called to a fact, which is not duly emphasized by most historians. Politics, as treated by the philosophers, was for a long time in the highest degree fashionable. Up to the highest circles the ladies took at least as lively an interest in them as the gentlemen, so that it was said the *salons* had become "little States-General." Here, however, the political discussions were principally looked upon as an animating pastime. One or two of the newly-founded clubs—an institution here-

[1] Rocquain, 298.   [2] Ib., 306.

tofore not known in France—betrayed some disposition to make them serve more serious purposes. But as yet they did not attract much public notice. The hot zeal with which the *bourgeoisie* plunged into the maëlstrom of political and social problems since Rousseau had thrust the firebrand of his impassionate dialectics into the mountains of venerable rubbish of every kind, could, however, not fail to strike even comparatively dull eyes as a sign of the times which ought not to be made light of. Upon the *bourgeoisie* his writings made the deepest impression, for it was the embittered plebeian that spoke to plebeians. And here again the disciples stood ready to outrun the master. The keenest observers were well aware of the fast growing desire of the *bourgeoisie* to try its hands at putting the theories of its great apostle into practice. As early as 1786, Mme. de Staël speaks of the "republican spirit of Paris." And the patriots had gone even beyond Rousseau. As theorists, they were less radical than he; but they were not only theorists, but also agitators, and as agitators they stepped into the midst of the vast masses that stood behind the *bourgeoisie*. Their weapons were not only books, but also pamphlets, and these pamphlets were written in such a way, that, as one of them expresses it, "the simplest and most uneducated people" could understand them. The seeds they sowed were slow to sprout. The surviving philosophers, proudly surveying their luxuriant harvest field, did not heed and hardly saw the little weeds cropping out here and there.[1] Their time came in the dog-days of the revolution, with their incessant alternation of scorching heat and torrents of rain..

The patriots had no successors. Lassitude sets in, says Rocquain. People amuse themselves and get over the gravest problems of the times by means of epigrams and lampoons. Did that mean that the winds had spent their force and everything had settled down to undisturbed rotting in utter stagnation? Just the opposite. The race is run, the work done. What this work was, is stated by Taine in two brief sentences: " All the insti-

[1] Grimm wrote in 1768 : "Cette lassitude générale du christianisme qui se manifeste de toutes parts, et particulièrement dans les Etats catholiques, cette inquiétude qui travaille sourdement les esprits et les porte à attaquer les abus religieux et politiques, est un phénomène caractéristique de notre siècle, comme l'esprit de réforme l'était du seizième, et présage une révolution imminente et inévitable. On peut dire que la France est le foyer de cette révolution, qui aura, sur les précédentes du moins, l'avantage de s'effectuer sans qu'il en coûte du sang."—V. 358, 359.

tutions have been sapped at the foundation. The reigning philosophy has withdrawn all authority from custom, from religion, and from the state."[1] I took exception to the assertion, that the literature of the 18th century is the primary cause of the revolution. It is more. It *is* the revolution— only in the abstract. And as early as 1770 the crown, in an official document published by express order of the king, formally admits, not that this revolution is *in process*, but that it has become an *accomplished* fact.[2] And while the philosophic revolution has completely broken down the *ancien régime* in the heads and in the hearts of the people, the *ancien régime*, according to Turgot, has resulted in the complete disintegration of the people.[3] The work of destruction had thus been done

---

[1] I. 302.

[2] Séguier, *avocat-général* of the Parliament of Paris, says in a *réquisitoire*, "Imprimé par ordre exprès du Roi," "Leur (the philosophers) objet était de faire prendre un autre cours aux esprits sur les institutions civiles et religieuses, et la révolution s'est pour ainsi dire opérée. Les royaumes ont senti chanceler leurs antiques fondements; et les nations, étonnées de trouver leurs principes anéantis, se sont demandé par quelle fatalité elles étaient devenues si différentes d'elles-mêmes."—Rocquain, 278.

[3] " La nation est une société composée de différents ordres mal unis, et d'un peuple dont les membres n'ont entre eux que très-peu de liens, et où, par conséquent, personne n'est

with equal thoroughness by the *ancien régime* itself and by the philosophers. Had the latter been as successful as to the positive side of their work? If not, what must the future be that was in store for France?

"Return to nature, *i. e.*, the abolishment of society, that is the war-cry of the whole encyclopædistic battalion," says Taine.[1] Yes, the abolishment not merely of this particular form of society, called the *ancien régime*, but of society—that is what the return to nature meant. Rousseau himself, while insisting upon it, that the organization of the commonwealth [2] must be absolutely determined by nature, very correctly says in one of his innumerable self-contradictions, that the constitution of the commonwealth is the work of art.[3] Because to them everything in the *ancien régime* seems to run directly counter to nature, the philosophers come to think that to find out what the proper political structure would be, all one has to

occupé que de son intérêt particulier. Nulle part il n'y a d'intérêt commun visible."

[1] I. 289.

[2] That is the proper rendering of *société*, as he understands the term.

[3] "La constitution de l'homme est l'ouvrage de la nature ; celle de l'Etat est l'ouvrage de l'art."—Contrat social, Livre III., ch. 11.

do is to reason the problem out logically from the nature of man as the given premises. That by this process at best the proper political structure for *abstract* man can be arrived at, they fail to see. They ignore the fact that in the real world institutions are always the product of historical evolution, and that therefore the "what *is*" cannot with impunity be left out of consideration, if in regard to a real people and with a view to practical application the "what *ought* to be" is to receive a satisfactory answer. They do not realize, that in the real world it is in itself a monstrous undertaking of a sudden to set up abstract reason and justice as the supreme lawgivers, because the real world cannot will the fact out of existence that it is what it is, *i. e.*, what it has grown to be, and cannot start out afresh, as if it were only now coming into existence. At least as to the task they have laid down for themselves they hold history in sovereign contempt. They not only ignore the facts, but to an astounding degree the insane, "So much the worse for the facts," is virtually their maxim.

But, it will be asked, how can this with justice be laid to their charge, if they do not at all pretend to deal with the facts, but declare their only purpose to be to establish the correct doctrine? At this moment I can give but one-half of my answer to this question. Their sovereign disregard of the facts necessarily becomes a source of incalculable mischief, because they themselves argue from beginning to end, as if their premises were incontestable and uncontested facts, while they are in truth but unproved and unprovable hypotheses. They assume a prehistoric state of nature of an impossible character, and make this the basis of their logical structure. This must crash down from top to bottom, if the basis be "a false creation, proceeding from the heat-oppressed brain."

To test the doctrine, it is fair to examine it in its last phase of evolution.

In the state of nature, ere society has come into existence, says Rousseau, all men have equal rights and the rights of every one are unbounded. Putting the alleged axiomatic truth into other words it reads thus: originally all have the fulness of nothing, for all are declared to have had equally unbounded rights at the time when no rights existed, the very conception of right not having as yet entered man's mind.[1] A feat of

[1] "'Jure enim naturali ab initio omnes homines liberi nascebantur;' which is equivalent to saying that before any

equal logical monstrosity is required for the next step forward. In the state of nature, says Rousseau expressly, man was "a stupid and dull animal"; the creating of society by the social contract "made him an intelligent being and a man."[1] Let it pass, that a contract presupposes law, is it not a most marvellous idea, to evolve intelligent men from dull animals by letting these dull animals simultaneously and unanimously perform an act of volition requiring the whole intellectual outfit of this great philosopher of the 18th century of the Christian era? To get the effect it is made the cause, and then the effect caused by itself, becomes the cause of all the rest, working strictly according to the precepts of implacable logic.

laws were in existence, no differences between man and man were recognized by law. Ulpian's 'jus naturale' is therefore a merely metaphorical phrase, leading to consequences which, however magniloquently they may be expressed, turn out upon analysis to be dangerous truisms. All legal right and wrong had its origin after human society was put in motion and began to reflect and act. To talk of law and right as applied to mankind at a supposed period anterior to society beginning to think and act is a contradiction in terms."—Th. E. Holland, The Elements of Jurisprudence, p. 32. "Das Recht existirt erst vermoege der Sanction der Rechtsgemeinschaft des einzelnen Staates."—Bar, Das internationale Privat-und Strafrecht, p. 519.

[1] Contrat social, Livre I., ch. 8.

And Rousseau not only rears his structure upon an imaginary basis, but he also builds it of imaginary material. In common with all the philosophers, he starts from the following two propositions: man is by nature reasonable, and, man is by nature virtuous. As to the first, Alexander Hamilton was unquestionably right, when he said: man is rather a reasoning than a reasonable animal. As to the second—well, why has it always been, why is it still, why will it remain to the end of days, such an arduous task to advance a step in making the life of mankind in state and society conform to the behests of ethics? Ah, the day was dawning that was to put the truth of the two assertions to an appalling test. The two together substituted for real man with his needs, desires, and passions, with his prejudices and bedimmed intellect, with his love and his hate, a soulless and heartless *homunculus*—for the ever falling, but still onward and upward striving man of God Almighty, the constructive being of the philosopher's brain, as mouldable by institutions as clay in the potter's hands. The judgeships, not requiring any special talents, says Rousseau, might be filled by drawing lots, for " good sense, justice, and integrity" are "common to all citizens in a well-constituted State;"[1] and Condorcet announces the day when reason will be the only master of man.[2] The philosophers—and, above all, Rousseau—were in fact but dreaming poets in the garb of stern logicians, fancying that by their dialectic juggleries they were elevating politics to the rank of a science, nay, laying the flattering unction to their soul, that they had—as Siéyès directly asserts—"*completed* the science of politics."[3]

Bachaumont makes a statement in regard to Rousseau's Social Contract, which the student of the history of the revolution must ponder well. "It only develops maxims," says the writer of the Secret Memoirs, "which everybody has in his heart."[4] This explains the almost unparalleled

---

[1] Contrat social, Livre IV., ch. 4.

[2] "Il arrivera donc ce moment où le soleil n'éclairera plus sur la terre que des hommes libres, ne reconnaissant pour maître que leur raison: où les tyrans et les esclaves, les prêtres et leurs stupides ou hypocrites instruments n'existeront plus que dans l'histoire et sur les théâtres."—Tableau des progrès de l'esprit humain. Dixième époque. Taine, I. 302.

[3] He adds: "The alleged historical truths have no more reality than the alleged religious truths." That goes far towards explaining how an accurate mind, like that of the renowned *abbé*, could be betrayed into raising such an insane pretension.

[4] I. 137.

success of the treatise : Rousseau only put into words what was in everybody's mind already. For the same reason, however, there was a terrible danger lurking in these pages. The spark of his terse, impassionate eloquence had kindled a fire, which needed but some wind to burst out into a blaze of fierceness, which nothing could check, for his logic seemed absolutely unanswerable to well-nigh all his contemporaries, and especially to those with whom those maxims had not been thoughts, but only vague sentiments, until he clad them in his inimitable language. Nothing is easier than to prove from Rousseau's writings that he thought, what Siéyès most explicitly declared : I do not propose to put my doctrines into practice ; it is the administrator's business to see how far that can be done ; the philosopher's duty is to tell the whole truth—to go to the end of the road.[1] But when the philosophers or their

---

[1] Au moins, dira-t-on, ce sont là des choses absolument impracticables par le temps qui court. Aussi je ne me charge point de les pratiquer. Mon rôle, à moi, et celui de tous les écrivains patriotes ; il consiste à publier la vérité. D'autres s'en rapprocheront plus ou moins, selon leur force et selon les circonstances, ou bien s'en écarteront par mauvaise foi, et alors nous souffrirons ce que nous ne pouvons pas empêcher.... Je rencontre partout de ces gens qui, par modération, voudraient *détailler* la vérité, ou n'en présenter

disciples had themselves become the administrators, would they then still see with equal distinctness the essential difference between the tasks of the two? Above all, would the crowd reason thus, when its notions had, actually and legally, become an authoritative power? Would then its coarser logic not assert itself, bluntly declaring: What *ought* to be, *must* be? And how could this conclusion be refuted? Did the Social Contract not proclaim in trumpet tones, as the very cornerstone of the whole edifice the maxim, that whatever is not in conformity with its tenets is illegal, null, and void—cannot, in the nature of things, be binding upon any one? Did it not expressly declare that the commonwealth itself had no right to, nay, cannot for prudential reasons, abate this principle by a hair's-breadth—that the slightest infraction, of itself dissolves the social contract, and restores everybody to the liberty of the state

à la fois que de légères parcelles. Je doute qu'ils s'entendent lorsqu'ils parlent ainsi. A coup sûr, ils ne considèrent pas assez la différence des obligations imposées à l'administrateur et au philosophe. Le premier s'avance comme il peut ; pourvu qu'il ne sorte pas du bon chemin, on n'a que des éloges à lui donner. Mais ce chemin doit avoir été percé jusqu'au bout par le philosophe. Il doit être arrivé au terme, sans quoi il ne pourrait garantir que c'est véritablement le chemin qui y mène."—Qu'est-ce que le Tiers-Etat? Edition Chapuys-Montlaville, Paris, 1839, p. 182.

of nature?[1] Was it then not the paramount duty of all and every one to avert this direst of all calamities? Could that be accomplished by reason and virtue? Oh, yes, of course; but reason and virtue must be enforced. Who will have a right to complain? Is it not the essence of the social contract that, as Rousseau says, " the general will *forces* everybody to be free "?[2] Ay, is to cry out against force and to pretend that it can be abused not to denounce oneself a rotten limb, which must be lopped off? For hear the infallible expounder of the miracles worked by the original contract concluded by the dull animals: " It is impossible that the whole should want to harm all its members; and we shall see, later on, that it cannot harm any one in particular. The sovereign (*i. e.*, the people) is, by the fact in itself of his existing, always what he ought to be."[3] Add to this the fundamental maxim, that the social contract consists in " the total alienation of each associate with all his rights to the community in the aggregate," and you will readily see what

---

[1] Livre I., ch. 6.
[2] " Quiconque refusera d'obéir à la volonté générale, y sera contraint par tout le corps : ce qui ne signifie autre chose sinon qu'on le forcera à être libre." Livre I., ch. 7.
[3] Ib.

evil genii could be conjured up out of these pages, when the masses, under the leadership of purblind doctrinarians and unscrupulous demagogues, became the authoritative interpreters of them, and passion run mad ruled the hour. If such a thing is conceivable as the most ruthless and unbounded despotism decked out with all the paraphernalia of unrestricted liberty, then here was its catechism.

But perhaps the writings of the other philosophers furnished some antidote to the poison that might be eventually extracted from those of Rousseau? If none could be found in them, it was not because they had confined themselves to tearing down and refrained from building up. Everybody took a hand in the agreeable business of setting the wicked world to rights. "There is to-day," writes Grimm in August, 1774, "not a young man who does not, upon leaving college, form a project of establishing a new system of government, not an author who does not consider himself obliged to teach the powers of the earth the best manner of directing their states."[1] Ten years before, however, he had written with regard to the same phenomenon: "From the pres-

[1] VIII. 383.

ence of many physicians one can infer that the patient is in a bad condition, and the moment when everybody volunteers his advice is usually that of the agony."[1] The trouble was, that to all the concoctions applied, what Voltaire, criticising one of the numberless financial pamphlets, says in the same year (1764) in characterization of all the philosophers: "Very successful in breaking down the systems of their adversaries and not establishing a better one." But what could it have helped anyhow to construct a better one, if Bachaumont was correct, and Rousseau had only said what was in everybody's mind already?

The *ancien régime* a whitewashed tomb, the leaders of public opinion riveting afresh the chains of the inherited belief in the omnipotence of legislation, and as stock in trade for effecting the imperative reorganization of state and society, nothing but impracticable theories, which readily lend themselves to most portentous perversions in the attempt to put them into practice—that was the awful situation of France. Surely it would have required a miraculous interposition of Providence to avert from her the days, whose legend Mme. Roland proclaimed in mounting the scaffold: "Oh Liberty, what crimes are committed in thy name!"

[1] III. 285.

LECTURE V.

A Typical Family Tragedy of Portentous Political Import.

" Don't be frightened! " It is said that on March 9th, 1749, these ill-omened words announced to Victor Riquetti, Marquis Mirabeau, that the longed for son and heir was born to him. The warning was to prepare him to see a twisted foot and an over-sized head of uncommon ugliness, rendered the more impressive by two premature teeth. If a prophet's hand had lifted for him the curtain concealing the future, he would have seen that there were other and infinitely graver reasons to frighten him. With that ill-shaped baby Providence had committed to his hands a trust of incalculable import to France and thereby to the world. He knew it no more than the child knew that the very first thing it did in life was to cause deep vexation to its irritable father by its unsightliness. If he had known it, he might have understood his duty towards the child somewhat differently, and some of history's most awful pages might possibly have a somewhat different tale to tell.

In his last years Mirabeau rather prided himself upon his ugliness. He declared it no mean element in his extraordinary power over men, and there was in fact a strange fascination in its forceful impressiveness. The father, however, was proof against its charm. If I read the character of the eccentric man correctly, the baby acted most unwisely in furnishing good cause for that horrified exclamation. Any father's child is to be pitied that is bid such a welcome upon its entrance into the world, and if there was a father whose feelings could not with impunity be trifled with, it was the famous author of the " Friend of Men." Forsooth a proud title. A brighter diadem than a crown, if it had been conferred by others. Bestowed by himself it savored of presumption. Still it was by no means a false, mendacious pretension. A great and warm heart beat with an uncommonly strong pulse in the rugged chest. But when this heart set to reasoning, as it was fearfully prone to do whenever it was hurt, it always did so with the sledge-hammer's logic. And as to this baby it at once began to reason, because it was deeply wounded in a most tender spot by its extravagant ugliness. From the first dismayed look the father took at his offspring, it was certain, that, unless the son proved a paragon of all virtues according to the father's conceptions, fair weather would be the exception rather than the rule in their relations. Ere the child is fairly out of the nursery they begin to take a tragical turn. When Gabriel Honoré is still a lithe-limbed boy, a veritable tragedy is well under way. The beard does not yet sprout on the chin of the youth, and bitter wrangling degenerates into a fierce feud. The same blood flows in their veins, but as to each other every drop of it seems to turn into corrosive poison. No diseased imagination of a sensational novelist has ever invented a wilder romance and used more glaring colors in painting characters and scenes. It is indescribably revolting, but at the same time of overwhelming heart-rending pathos, not only because it is life and not fiction, but principally because both, father and son, are infinitely more to be pitied than to be blamed, though the guilt of both is great. As to this there can be no difference of opinion. But for more than a century it has been a much controverted question, whether the father or the son was the more culpable. I shall give no doubtful answer to the question, as to what I think on this head. By far the greater stress, however, I lay on the assertion, that the principal culprit was the *ancien régime.* If this be not made the basal line in examining the case, it is impossible to do full justice to either of the parties, and, in my opinion, all the historians of the portentous family tragedy have thus far more or less failed to see or, at least, to do this.

Unless Marquis Victor could exempt himself from the law that causes have effects, his being constantly in hot water in regard to his family affairs was inevitable. The hot sun of the Provence tells upon the temperature of the blood, and with the Mirabeau it seemed to rise a degree or two with every generation. In this respect nothing was changed by the fact that any ordinary man would have died if he had lost half the quantity of blood that flowed in the wars of Louis XIV. from the wounds of Jean Antoine, Victor's father. He deemed it his due always to be sent where death was sure to reap the richest harvest, and he was not possessed of any charm rendering him steel-and-bullet-proof. Of one of the battles he used to speak as " the day on which I died." The soldiers said of him: "He is a Mirabeau; they are all devils."

Victor and his brothers were genuine scions of old Jean Antoine. One of them, known in later years as the *bailli*, was to play an important part in the life of the great revolutionist. In his character is much less base alloy than in that of any other member of the family. He is by far the most estimable and sympathetic of them all. And yet even he had passed through a period, when it seemed infinitely more likely that he would end in some drunken brawl as a disgrace to his family, than that he would render the name "illustrious," as Victor could with some justice aver he had done. Jean Antoine, the younger, had not been reformed by being branded and treated as an irredeemable criminal; one fine day he had of his own accord turned over a new leaf. The marquis commended the sagacity of the superiors in allowing the better self of the young officer time to assert itself.[1] Would that he had learned something

---

[1] " Je connais ma tempestive race. J'ai vu, en quelque sorte, la jeunesse du bailli qui, pendant trois ou quatre ans, ne passait pas quatre jours de l'année hors de la prison ; et, sitôt qu'il voyait le jour, courait se perdre d'eau-de-vie, et de là tomber sur le corps de tout ce qu'il trouvait en son chemin, jusqu'à ce qu'on l'abattît et le portât en prison. Mais, avec

from this lesson in regard to the treatment of his son!

It is the more astonishing that it was utterly lost upon him, because he did not even need to recall to his memory the turbulent youth of the beloved brother to know, that no Mirabeau was in his youth a candidate for sainthood; that upon every Mirabeau a strong curb acted as a maddening lash, and that though the Mirabeaus were lamentably liable to be for a while appallingly familiar with the gutter, they never made it their permanent abode and might be depended upon being ultimately worth a good deal more than most of those who had never tripped into it. He himself bears loud testimony to the fact that his own story is a pretty eloquent sermon on this threefold text. " Women," he confessed, " were the only occupation of my foolish youth;" and, "licentiousness became my second nature."[1] And yet he had even a much better right to declare in the same sentence in which he said his brother had

cela, il avait de l'honneur à l'excès, et ses chefs, gens experimentés alors, promettaient toujours à ma mère qu'il serait un jour excellent. Cependant, personne ne pouvait l'arrêter et il s'arrêta tout-à-coup de lui-même."—The marquis to the count du Saillant, Jan. 26, 1770. Lucas Montigny: Mémoires de Mirabeau, I. 293, 294.

[1] Alfred Stern, Das Leben Mirabeaus, I. 12.

rendered the name "illustrious," that he had made it "famous" (*célèbre*). Yes, his drinking so deeply from the cup of lust did not prevent his settling down to earnest work and becoming one of the celebrities of the times. And deservedly so. There are to-day competent judges who think that the contemporaries under- rather than over-estimated him. He was one of the foremost founders of the new school of national economists, called Physiocrats. Partly he even anticipated Quesnay, the celebrated physician of Mme. Pompadour, who is always named as the originator of the new doctrines. "The Friend of Men" was not only a keen, but also an independent and very original thinker. Among the discoveries of the all-pervading interdependence of material and moral conditions, he stands in the very first rank as to time, clearness of perception, and systematic examination.

I doubt whether the great truth was revealed to him by abstract reasoning and observation, though he was an acute reasoner and a good observer. Moralizing is the dominant tract of his character. It is with him not only a strong tendency, but a burning, irrepressible, and uncontrollable passion. One would have to search long among his innumerable letters to find a single one that does not betray it in some way or other. I am, therefore, inclined to suppose that while the abstract thinker and the observer furnished abundant materials to the moralist, the moralist had primarily led the abstract thinker and the observer on the right way.

But however that be, the three necessarily conspired to push him in many respects of the highest moment into conscious and sharp antagonism to the *ancien régime*. Unfeigned broad humanitarianism, inborn aversion to all sham and hollow pretence, the honest desire to grasp the essence of things, coupled with the truthful intention to conform his feeling, thinking, and acting to it, and a morbid pleasure in fault-finding, served to impart a piquant democratic flavor to the pungent censures of the critic as well as to the doctrines of the enthusiastic apostle. And yet no man held the levelling heresies of democracy in greater horror than he. He was not only an unquestioning believer in the theory of the blue blood, but he made an idol of it and worshipped at its shrine with the passionate devotion of an Eastern fanatic. It was in his nature to delight in posing as implacable justice incarnate, and to use in this rôle, instead of the anachronistic bandage of the stern goddess, a magnifying glass of extraordinary power. But if in the code, according to which he pronounced sentence, the chapter on his obligations towards his ancestors had not held such a prominent place, he would after all have been a more lenient, and therefore better and much wiser father.

There is a highly respectable element in this: a deep-rooted spirit of loyalty. But like everything else in this singular man it is ill-balanced. Where it remains unshaken, as towards his old mother,[1] it is pushed to reprehensible excess: "She was to me God on earth," he writes to the Marquis Longo.[2] Where it is overcome by just resentment, as towards his wife, his eldest son, and one of his daughters, it still asserts itself by lashing him into such a fury, that by dint of reasoning under the

---

[1] She did not take kindly to her elder grandson. The marquis' idolatrous veneration for her seems to render it likely that this also influenced his feeling towards the boy. Montigny says she "avait de l'aversion pour l'ainé."—Mém., VIII. 80. Her favorite was the marquis' younger son, best known by his nickname Mirabeau-Tonneau. He had made an excellent record as a valiant officer in the American war of independence. In the National Assembly he was one of his great brother's political antipodes in the ultra-conservative faction. He excelled more by sarcastic wit than by sound judgment.

[2] May 22, 1779. Mém., III. 458.

dictation of his lacerated heart, the moralist is turned into a moral monstrosity. The intrepid and high-minded arraigner of despotism deems it his incontestable right before God and man to be sole and irresponsible judge, though he is a party to the case, and he glories in making his heart a flint against the supplications of the son;[1] he fairly dotes on the savage cruelties in which he vengefully indulges, complacently dubbing them just punishments; nay, he has the infernal courage to present another daughter, the best beloved of his children, with a pen-portrait of the wife that had borne him eleven children, every line of which appealed to her to despise, if not to curse the womb that had borne her.[2] And this man declared again and again emphatically and in perfect good faith, that

[1] When Mirabeau had succeeded—not without difficulty—in sending to him from the Donjon de Vincennes a letter of hot entreaties, he did not deign to take any notice of it whatever. To the *bailli* he wrote concerning this letter: " La lettre m'eût-elle touché, effleuré même, il n'en serait ni plus, ni moins de ma façon de penser, et du plan de conduite qui est à poste fixe dans mon âme et dans ma conscience, que j'aurais dans tous les cas, vis-à-vis de ce personnage, parce que tout est fondé sur l'idée très-réfléchie de mon devoir ; mais cette lettre n'a fait ni l'un ni l'autre, et je le laisse sur le fumier de ses crimes."—June 3, 1779. Mém., II. 305.

[2] He calls her in this letter " in every respect an unmitigated monster."

he had never crossed any one's way, nor ever done the slightest harm to anybody.[1]

In our times such a character would be in any civilized country an impossibility. At all times the germs of the same discordant traits may be found in many bosoms. But even where much less resistance is offered by the good qualities, laws, customs, and public opinion so effectively restrain the development of the evil ones, that they seldom force themselves at all upon the attention of the superficial observer. In the *ancien régime* everything tended to nurse them into luxuriant growth, and Marquis Victor, in spite of his being "the Friend of Men," was as genuine a son of the *ancien régime* as could be found in France. He is a representative of the doomed old, as well as of the dawning new spirit of the times. In spite of their being indissolubly blended in

---

[1] In a letter of March 30, 1769, to the *bailli*, he says of himself: "Qui est l'ami de tous ceux qui ne l'ont jamais vu; qui, par lui-même ni par son ombre, n'a jamais été sur le chemin de qui que soit; qui n'a jamais fait peur, ni embarras, ni mal à personne."—Mém., I. And while he kept the son "buried alive" in the Donjon de Vincennes, he wrote: "Je n'ai jamais fait ni voulu faire du mal à personne: cependant, je semble être un objet du courroux du ciel, et dans tous les details, et de toutes les manières."—Oct. 21, 1778. Mém., II. 296.

him, they constantly contend with each other for the mastery, and, as to his family relations, the former always carries the day. His severest accusers are his strong redeeming features. It is easier to forgive a monster than a more than highly respectable man, a man with traits of real intellectual and moral grandeur, who acts like a monster towards his nearest kin. It is in vain to search for any other excuse than that afforded by the only possible explanation of it: he was the product of a monstrous state of society.

It is hard to decide whom he made to suffer the most from it. I rather think it was himself, not, however, because his heart bled, as it unquestionably did, but because his pride was wounded unto death. His heart, so far from being destitute of feeling, was morbidly sensitive; [1] but to minister

[1] He writes, Nov. 13, 1759, to the Comtesse de Rochefort: "Vous savez que mon tendon d'Achille est dans le cœur— un cœur qui sent les peines, les pressent, les divine, les anticipe." And he declares to be "de plus en plus persuadé de mon grand principe moral, qui est que pour travailler à son propre bonheur ici-bas, il faut sans cesse cultiver la sensibilité et déraciner l'amour-propre."—Mém., I. 258. There was a good deal of truth in this self-characterization. The trouble was that, as I said before, he allowed his heart to do his thinking. "Je dois te le dire, le cœur pense beaucoup trop chez toi," scolds the *bailli*, who was of a much kindlier disposition. (Ib., III. 342.) And the marquis himself very

to his pride he did not shrink from crushing his heart, and his pride was the typical pride of the nobleman of the *ancien régime*.

He was not contented with his family being one of the foremost of the Provence; he was bent upon making it one of the great families of France. The hot zeal and the recklessness, with which he began to work at the realization of this proud fancy, became the bane of his life. Literally and figuratively he was made to pay a fearful price for it. It was the foundation on which he reared with wonderful skill the gorgeous structure of his family's misery, shame, and guilt.

Though he was ever hunting for wealth, and contentions about money were one of the principal causes of the interminable and fierce family feuds, he does not seem to have had any craving for money for its own sake. Nor was he addicted to an ostentations and luxurious way of living. First that dream of his ambition, and then the ever-

correctly said: "Le sentiment est souvent mauvais logicien." (Ib., III. 444.) He added: "Mais jamais trompeur sciemment." That is only half true. There is such a thing as conscious self-deception in regard to one's feelings. The *ancien régime* had made it so common a fault, that it became one of the most characteristic and most portentous traits of the spirit of the times, and the marquis was uncommonly skilled in the cunning craft.

increasing embarrassments growing out of it were at the bottom of it all. Even to his many speculative ventures was he prompted as much by that aspiration, as by the desire to put his economic theories to the test of practice. Not one of them stood it under his management.

" Your fine plans often looked to me, as if they were built upon the mists of the Seine,"[1] grumbled the good-natured *bailli*, who had an almost unbounded admiration for the elder brother, and again and again put his hand deep into his own pocket to keep him afloat. As the marquis himself as early as 1766 figured out that he had sunk at least 200,000 francs in the incidental expenses alone of his ventures, the reproach was certainly not wholly unfounded.[2] But the good *bailli*, as he complained, was never believed in time, no more in questions of this than of any other kind.[3] How should or could he? The marquis always did what his duty bade him do, and he was not the man to compromise with his duty to please any one.

[1] Stern, I. 18.
[2] " En frais de notaires, de courtage, de banque, etc."— Letter of Oct. 29, 1766, to the *bailli*. Mém., I. 221.
[3] "Tu ne m'as de ta vie cru à temps, quoique tu aies souvent dit que le bailli avait toujours raison."—July 15, 1783. Mém., III. 375.

As to his living in Paris and the bad speculations, the brother, however, accused him of always managing "to make his duties conform to his tastes."[1] In other and graver questions, strange to say, they always accorded, if not exactly with his tastes, at least with what he, under the circumstances, liked best to do. That was hardly fortunate, for the man who protested that he had never crossed the way of any one also frankly declared: "I am headstrong as a woman in child-bed is brave."[2] Surely, to be an object of his duties was to run no small risk. A man who justly boasts of being the blindly obedient slave of his conscience is certain to be the terror of others, if the behests of his conscience so miraculously happen to coincide with what his notions and passions prompt him to do. In one of his lucid moments in regard to himself, he confesses that he could hardly have selected an unsafer guide than this odd conscience of his. "I have almost always exaggerated and misplaced my conscience," he writes to the *bailli*.[3]

It was all the more a dangerous guide, because— as the *bailli* said—he was "possessed of the devil

---

[1] Nov. 28, 1782. Mém., III. 323.
[2] Nov. 12, 1776, to the Marquis Longo. Mém., III. 444.
[3] Dec. 20, 1782. Mém., I. 236; III. 325.

of scribomania."[1] He never allowed the ink in his pen to get dry, always wrote what he felt or thought at the moment, expressed it always in the most drastic words his perfervid imagination could command, and—his implacable conscience ever presiding over his counsels—was very loth to retract anything he had said. Thus his pen necessarily became a most fruitful source of mischief.[2] For there was in his moods and, consequently, in his momentary opinions and judgments, no more stability than in an April sky, and he was possessed not only of the devil of scribomania, but also of the arch-devil of "the fanaticism of infallibility," as Montigny expresses himself. The great moralist Vauvenargues wrote to him: "You are fiery, spiteful, stormier, prouder, and more changeable than the sea, thirsting above all for pleasure, knowledge, and honors."[3] Now look at the power accorded by the laws and customs to

[1] Mém., III. 355.
[2] "Ta plume, après t'avoir attiré bien des chagrins, est ce qui rend cette réunion (of Mirabeau and his wife) si difficile ; et, en vérité, on te prend de partout sur tes écrits quelconques ; et tous les malheurs ont distillé de ta plume, parce que tu as écrit toute la vie suivant la pensée du moment, sans réfléchir que les circonstances changeant, les idées peuvent et doivent même changer."—Mém. III., 342. 343.
[3] Stern, I. 13.

a man—and he a nobleman of eminence and influence—over his family, remember that the *ancien régime* was simply paternalism run mad, recollect that Marquis Victor was a most genuine son of the *ancien régime*, and you can form some idea of the temptations and possibilities for tyranny offered to an infallible man, stormier and more changeable than the sea, and implicitly obeying a conscience, that is at the same time so complacent, so exacting, and so rigorous.

The marquis was none of your shilly-shallying votaries of paternal duty. Ere he began to look about for a wife, his irrepressible pen was busy laying down the law for his children that were to be. When he chose a wife, he did so solely with a view to making the next Marquis Mirabeau one of the bulky planets in the solar system of monarchical France. He had, as it appears, never seen Miss Vassan before setting out on the journey for his nuptials. But what of that? No sentimentalities in business, and he was among the nobility of France no exception to the rule in looking upon marriage purely as a business affair. In the uppermost layer of society, a marriage merely from love, and a pure and happy matrimonial life were much commented upon with a sort of puzzled admiration, but the contrary was too common to call for any other notice than as a legitimate subject of social small talk.[1] Miss Vassan, to judge from her portrait, was not the ogre the marquis afterwards tried to make her out; but she was no beauty either. What was under her skin, it would be time enough to find out after the nuptial knot was tied. About her being a rich heiress there was no doubt, and this was for the present so much the only question of moment, that the marquis even refrained from higgling about some objectionable clauses in the marriage contract, rather than to defer making sure of the fine prize against all peradventure.

When husband and wife were afterwards fighting each other in and out of the courts like two wild cats, the marquis declared in his emphatic style, that his amiable spouse had kept him for some twenty years in nephritic colic. The fact that she had borne him eleven children sufficiently proves

[1] "Sur vingt seigneurs de la cour, il y en a quinze qui ne vivent point avec leurs femmes et qui ont des maîtresses. Rien même n'est si commun à Paris entre particuliers."—Barbier, IV. 496. "Jamais ils (husband and wife) ne se voyaient, jamais on ne les rencontrait dans la même voiture, jamais on ne les trouvait dans la même maison, ni, à plus forte raison, réunis dans un lieu public."—De Besenval, 49. Quoted by Taine, I. 172.

the monstrosity of the exaggeration. But to conclude from this fact, that, in the main, the relations between them must have been for many years pretty much what they ought to have been, would nevertheless be a great mistake. Loyalty and pride induced the marquis for a long time determinedly to shut his own eyes against his misery. The *bailli* repeatedly told him in later years: Your putting on a serene face never deceived any one but yourself.

The marquise was uneducated, of little intellectuality, ill-mannered, slovenly, fickle, passionate, blindly yielding to every impulse, moody and wilful, shockingly indiscreet and grossly sensual. We have heard what the marquis had to report of himself on the latter score. Fierce, unrestrainable sensualism was one of the principal curses blighting Mirabeau's life.[1] The father, judging his son on this head, certainly had no right to forget that he owed his existence to gross sensualism wedded to gross sensualism.

The marquise being possessed of so many amiable qualities and the marquis being endowed

---

[1] He wrote to Champfort: "As to women I am the weakest of all men. I have idolized them and, if this be possible, my spiritual being can do even less without one than my physical."—Quoted by Stern, I. 170.

with Job's temper, the family life, of course, became every year more and more heaven on earth. Already in 1758 separation was talked of. Four years later some letters, convicting his wife of adultery, accidentally fell into the marquis' hands. Thereupon she had to comply with his demand, to relieve him of her hateful presence. Pride kept him from using this weapon in court, though the wife, turned into a raving fury, goaded him to madness by the violence and vileness of her attacks. When his consent was asked to have the suit of the son against his wife carried before the court of last resort, he refused it saying: the public were not to get from him a tragedy in five acts; he was not going to furnish them any fresh cause for saying: shall we never hear of anything but this ungovernable race?[1] It was, however,

[1] "Tu me demandes absolument de décider si je veux que l'on plaide *oui* ou *non* ; tu veux que je prononce, et je dis *non*, absolument *non*, quant à présent *non*. Je tiens par tous les bouts, mais je ne tiens qu'à des roseaux tranchans, à des branches épineuses, à des barreaux de fer rouge. Puisque le public aime les tragédies et les drames en cinq actes, qu'il aille en demander à Molé ; moi et les miens nous n'avons été, et ne sommes que trop en spectacle. Mon propre procès (against his wife) bruit encore, et je suis chaque jour braillé en pleine audience au palais ; je ne veux pas grossir ce cri universel: *n'entendrons-nous jamais parler que de cette race effrénée des Mirabeau ?*"—Jan. 27, 1788, to the *bailli*. Mém., III. 347, 348.

not only pride, that prevented him from purchasing victory over his wife at the price of letting the world know the worst. The marquise replied to his charges: "If any guilt attaches to me, it has grown entirely out of yours." Whether this counter-charge was well-founded as to the assertion of priority, cannot be said; but that the marquis was guilty of adultery was known to everybody, who knew anything at all about him.

Mme. de Pailly, the wife of a retired officer living in Switzerland, consoled him for having been so unlucky in the lottery of marriage. She was no common mistress. She was an ever welcome guest at some of the first families and sincerely respected by many highly estimable people. Even the stern piety of the marquis' old mother became reconciled to seeing the stranger occupy the place of legitimate wife at her son's fireside. If one wants to fathom the rottenness of this society, one must realize what it signifies, that even the best are stricken to such a degree with color-blindness as to some of the fundamental principles of social ethics. To these good people it seems the most natural thing to keep heaven snugly warm with the furnaces of hell. The marquis and Mme. de Pailly always scrupulously guarded appearances; she was well educated, refined, so entirely free from mercenary motives, that even her not over-well garnished purse was always at the disposal of the ever needy nobleman; she took an appreciative interest in his intellectual pursuits, advised him—only too readily—as to his unruly children, poured balm on his aching heart, tended him kindly in his bodily ailments, stood staunchly by him against neglect, envy, ingratitude, and calumny—surely that was more than sufficient to justify the pasting of a little slip of paper over that troublesome seventh commandment, or at least the interpreting it somewhat freely to suit one's convenience. The marquis died in the belief that, as never anything but bliss had come to him from his attachment to Mme. Pailly, the Almighty had not taken amiss the liberty he had taken in this respect with His behest. Others thought that he had been terribly punished for it. The *bailli* told him to his face that if it had not been for Mme. Pailly, his relations to his children would never have become such an infernal cesspool. He did not directly charge her with intentionally sowing tares, but he maintained that she had actually done so all the while, because the consciousness of being an illegitimate intruder rendered her all the more determined to hold exclusive and unlimited sway over him.[1]

[1] Loménie tells the story in a way calculated to produce the impression that this was but a passing notion, mainly due to Mirabeau's misrepresentations and persuasive eloquence. If he had given all the quotations bearing on this question, which Montigny furnishes from the *bailli's* correspondence, every unbiased reader would be convinced that such is not the case. The *bailli* knew that it was impossible to cure his infallible brother of his infatuation—he too was a true son of the times, holding altogether too lax opinions on such questions—love and admiration for his brother rendered him in this as in all other respects over-indulgent towards his faults and weaknesses—and he was fair-minded enough not to shut his eyes to the good qualities of the woman. These were the reasons why he now and then spoke in a different tone of her. To the unspectacled reader of his letters it is, however, as clear as anything can be, that his well-settled opinion accorded with the truth : he cursed the hour which had brought the marquis into contact with Mme. Pailly.—"Trop de gens se mêlent de tes affaires: tu me comprendras si tu veux ; que tout ce qui te parait obscur soit éclairci par toi-même, et point d'yeux étrangers, surtout des yeux féminins ; plus ces yeux-là ont d'esprit et sont aimables, plus il faut s'en méfier, comme de ceux d'une belle Circé, derrière laquelle l'esprit de domination et de jalousie s'établie et s'insinue, de manière que les plus grands hommes en sont les dupes ... celle (femme) en qui tu as une trop forte confiance est comme les autres, veut être la maîtresse: tout ce qui peut faire obstacle à cet empire, ou le partager, lui est désagréable, et en est haï cordialement. Règle générale, et sans exception, toute femme, dans sa position, veut gouverner absolument, et elle comme les autres ... ce ... choque beaucoup les enfans ; elle n'a jamais aimé aucun des tiens ... compte que, sans me mêler trop dans les choses, je vois à peu près tout, et je laisse

It was an uncommonly ugly baby—that is all I have thus far said of him who was to render the name Mirabeau immortal, and yet I have said already enough to decide the mooted question, whether the father or the son was more to blame, that the story of their relations was written with gall and venom and the latter's name became a stench in the nostrils of all decent people. I have said enough

aller, parce que je sais qu'on ne peut pas empêcher la rivière de couler."—" Faible dont tu ne guériras pas, parce que nos passions durcissent avec nos os, au lieu de décliner avec notre âge, soit dit en passant, car on te flatte et tu te flattes." Even if he (the marquis) owed her much more gratitude than he supposes, " il n'en est pas moins vrai qu'à mes yeux et à ceux de tous ceux qui prennent intérêt à la chose, quoique très-innocemment, et aveuglée elle-même sur les objets, certainement elle à causé beaucoup de mal à toi et à ta famille, car on ne me parlait jamais d'elle, qu'en ricanant, et tout le monde sentait que la jalousie de ton adverse (the wife) était placée. Tu es fort éloignée d'avoir procréé de ton corps des anges; mais tes enfans, eussent-ils été cela, jamais des enfans ne se verront gouverner et gourmer dans leur maison par une étrangère, fût-elle leur marâtre, sans en avoir du dépit." He is not to tell him, that she has never spoken " mordacement " to the children ; he himself has heard it and interfered. He does not want to deprive him of what offers him consolation. " Je veux croire que la personne en question n'a pas la méchanceté que lui supposent tous ceux qui l'ont vu vis-à-vis de tes enfans ; mais elle est femme, et veut commander, et suit mécaniquement son instinct." He renders her responsible for the fact that Mirabeau lost the suit against his wife.—Mém., III. 200, 201, 205, 206, 208, 409, 419.

to decide this question, unless one is prepared to contend that not parents have to educate their children, but children their parents, and to deny that example is one of the most essential elements in education.

Surely, the children of the marquis would have needed a treble set of guardian angels, to come out of the atmosphere of this household uncontaminated. As to Honoré a whole battalion of them would have been of no avail, for against them father and son were from the first the closest allies. All that was out of joint and awry in the father's way of feeling, thinking, and acting, was brought to bear upon the hapless child systematically, with dogged persistency, and the utmost force. Not enough that he was born so ugly that the most mealy-hearted father, intending to make his son the head of one of the great families of France, would have felt justly aggrieved. As if he wanted to try just how much the father's patience would stand, he became still more disfigured by small-pox. The *bailli* was informed that his nephew vied in ugliness "with the devil's nephew." Starting from this basis, the marquis soon commenced to discover that he resembled this disreputable personage in many other respects also. Small wonder! The precocious child was a most genuine twig of the old tree, and most people judge those defects of character with the greatest severity which characterize themselves. Upon the hot-tempered father afflicted with the infallibility-delusion and the duty-craze, the faithful reproduction of his own unconfessed faults in his son necessarily had the effect that a red cloth has upon the turkey-cock, and the logical consequence was a pedagogical policy necessarily producing results diametrically opposed to those it was intended to have. Dismay grew into chronic anger, baffled anger into provoking passion, thwarted passion into obdurate rigor and obstinacy, defied rigor into systematic injustice and cruelty breeding revengeful spite and more and more weakening and wrenching out of shape all the springs of moral volition.

The brain in the oversized head of the boy worked with unnatural intensity,[1] and molten iron instead of blood seemed to flow in his veins. What he needed above all was, therefore, a steady hand to guide him. The hand, however, cannot possibly be steady, if the judgment is constantly

---

[1] When he was five years old his father reported: "Whole Paris speaks of his knowledge."

whirling around like a weathercock. Now the father sees in him "a lofty heart under the jacket of a babe, with a strange but noble instinct of pride," and only four days later, he has changed into "a type of unutterably deep baseness, of absolute platitude, and the quality of an uncouth and dirty caterpillar, which will not undergo a transformation."[1] Then again: "An intelligence, a memory, a capacity which overpower, exciting astonishment, nay fright." And not quite four weeks later: "A nothing, embellished with trivialities, that will throw dust into the eyes of chatterboxes, but never be anything but a quarter of a man, if, peradventure, he should ever be anything at all."

Unquestionably, it was no easy task properly to educate this boy, for there was a great deal of solid foundation for every one of the father's contradictory judgments: the boy was like the father as "changeable as the sea." Still, by conforming the education with untiring, loving patience, to the strongly pronounced individuality of the child, a good pedagogue would have been sure to achieve excellent results. The application of any cut-and-

---

[1] I am at a loss to find a better rendering of the fine "qui ne se déchevelera pas."

dried system based upon preconceived notions was certain to work incalculable mischief. This the marquis failed to see, and his system was in all its parts as adapted to the intellectual and moral peculiarities of the boy, as a blacksmith's hammer to the repairing of a chronometer.

Many years later, the Baron Von Gleichen wrote to the father: "I told you often, that you would make a great rascal of the boy, while he was of a stuff to make a great man of him. He has become both."[1] So it was, and that he became a rascal was, to a great extent, due to the treatment he received at his father's hands, while he became a great man in spite of it. Appeals to reason, pride, honor, noble ambition, and, above all, affection, always awakened a strong responsive echo in his bosom;[2] the father, however, whenever he was

[1] Denkwürdigkeiten des Baron C. H. von Gleichen, 90. Quoted by Stern, I. 67.

[2] The father himself wrote with purblind self-complacency: "La rigueur ne lui (the writer) coûterait rien."—March 21, 1767. Mém., I. 287. Mirabeau, however, said: "Un Lambert pouvait me perdre, un Vioménil tout obtenir de moi."—Lettres de Vincennes, I. 295. Lambert commanded the regiment at Saintes, in which Mirabeau commenced his military service. The father had selected this regiment, because Lambert enjoyed the reputation of being the strictest disciplinarian in the army. Vioménil was the kindly colonel of the *légion de Lorraine* with which Mirabeau went to Corsica.

provoked—and the high-spirited unruly boy constantly provoked him—had only sternness, stinging sarcasm, sharp rebuke, and severe punishment for him. Instead of educating him by methodically developing his better qualities he persists in trying to subdue him by fear, although he cannot help confessing that the word fear is not to be found in the boy's vocabulary. Contradicting himself, he then again proudly asserts that, while Honoré is afraid of no one else, he fears him. That was a delusion. He knew that from the father he had to expect nothing but punishment, and that he tried to elude by hook and by crook, having, in spite of his fearlessness, no more a liking for it than any other boy. The father accused him, now and ever afterwards, of being by nature a liar. It was he who had caused the germ of untruthfulness, which is liable to be pretty strong with most very vivacious children, to sprout so vigorously and to cast such deep roots, by systematically watering it every day. From his early childhood to the day of his death, Mirabeau was possessed of a secret charm, that, in spite of everything, opened him the hearts of almost all people with whom he came into closer contact.[1] Even

[1] The father never tires of bitterly complaining about

the father was by no means, as he pretended to be, wholly proof against it.[1] But as he was extraordinarily skilful in deceiving himself on this head, he also admirably succeeded in concealing it from the son. The boy learned more and more to look upon his father as his one natural enemy, whom it was a matter of course to oppose by all available means, fair and foul. He did his best to make himself a terror to his son, and he not only deadened natural affection, but also undermined filial respect. To reimpose the punishments remitted by the teacher,[2] to make everybody, from the father-

---

that. "N'eût-il que son horrible talent pour faire des dupes, il ne serait bon qu'à étouffer : un homme, marchand de Dijon, disait à Gassaud : ' Il m'emporte beaucoup, mais tout ce que j'ai serait encore à son service.' "—" Le marquis de Lambert me disait l'autre jour qu'il avait partagé la ville et la province entre la raison et lui, et que, malgré son caractère odieux, il aurait trouvé dans la ville de Saintes vingt mille livres qui n'y sont pas."—" Il ensorcelle le bailli d'Aulan lui-même."—" C'est à ne savoir à qui entendre dans ce concert de panégyristes."—"Votre frère avait gagné tout le pays, peuple, et les bons juges ; il est étonnant comme ce bourreau-là s'empare de tout le monde."—Mém., I. 298, 300 ; III. 344, 412.

"Tant qu'Honoré a été avec toi, tu m'en a chanté les louanges, quoique avec la retenue que le passé inspirait. Depuis que tu ne l'as vu, on l'a fait redevenir à tes yeux un homme terrible."—The *bailli* to the marquis, Dec. 25, 1782. Mém., III. 345.

[2] " Monsieur le comte ne sort pas de sa suite de pénitences ;

confessor down to the comrades, a spy and informant,[1] purposely and confessedly to exaggerate to instructors and superiors his moral shortcomings [2]— that was a policy to drive an angel to revolt. It would have been nothing less than a miracle, if it had not goaded into viciousness an unusually bright and hot-tempered boy, with a superabundance of human nature in his every fibre.[3] There is no surer way utterly to ruin a full-blooded colt than madly to tear and jerk the bridle, while brutally belaboring him with spur and whip.

et, en vérité, il en a et en mérite prou. Je suis un instrument de plus pour Poisson (the tutor), parce que, quand il a promis rémission, je lui sers à y manquer, sans manquer sa parole, et je tiens rigeur."—Oct. 10, 1756. Mém., I. 248.

[1] Honoré "me parait, du moins jusqu'à ce temps, ne devoir être qu'un fou, presque invinciblement maniaque, en sus de toutes les qualités viles de sa souche maternelle. Comme il va maintenant chez nombre de maîtres choisis, et que, depuis le confesseur jusqu'au camarade, tout est autant de correspondans qui m'informent, je vois le naturel de la bête et je ne crois pas qu'on en fasse jamais rien de bon."—Apr. 19, 1763. Mém., I. 273.

[2] "J'ai pris le véritable tour pour l'engager (a certain Sigrais, to whose care he committed Honoré), non seulement en ne lui cachant rien, mais encore en chargeant la mesure." —Jan. 15, 1764. Mém., I. 275.

[3] Mirabeau said of himself, "Il (mon cœur) est bon, mais fougueux ; mon esprit lui-même est mélangé de bien comme de mal. C'est mon imagination trop bouillante, trop impétueuse, et trop mobile qui a fait mes erreurs et mes fautes." —May 28, 1778. Mém., II. 309.

Honoré was still a child, and the marquis already persuaded himself that he was in the strict sense of the word a criminal. He not only said so, but he also treated him as such, though he admitted, that in truth thus far only boyish pranks could be laid to his charge.[1] As a last attempt to save him from perdition, he was, at the age of fifteen years, entrusted to the *abbé* Choquard.[2] The marquis himself applies to the institution the harsh name " reformatory school." It was not so bad as that. Among Honoré's comrades were even some English boys " of family," who were not at all suspected of being candidates for the hangman's kind attentions. Not by putting him into this institution did the marquis disgrace his son, but he did brand him by depriving him of his name. As Pierre Buffière he was entered in the lists. Loménie—*facile princeps* among Mirabeau's biographers—makes light of this. He is even strongly inclined to suppose that, as Buffière was the name of a large estate forming part of the

---

[1] Yet in 1771, he writes to Choiseul, " Qu'il n'a jamais pu étre noté que pour des travers d'enfance."—Loménie, III. 66.

[2] " Cet homme est roide, et force les punitions dans le besoin : ce dernier essai fait et rempli, s'il n'y a pas d'amendement, comme je n'en espére point," etc.—June 2, 1764, to the *bailli*. Mém., 276.

prospective inheritance of his wife, the marquis was largely induced by the desire to gratify his pride to impose this name upon the son.[1] A strange way of distributing light and shadow in painting this family tragedy! The marquis states in the plainest words, that he intends to burn a mark upon the forehead of the son, and with something of an ugly grin, he tells of the desperate but vain resistance of the boy to its application.[2] A chasm was torn open between father and son, which could never again be completely bridged over.

Here again Mirabeau soon gained the vivid affection, not only of his comrades, but also of his teachers. A touching demonstration of the former induced his father to refrain from carrying out the intention of punishing him for the crime of accepting some money presents from his mother, by taking him out of the school and casting him adrift on the sea of life in a way which would

---

[1] Loménie, III. 213.

[2] Je n'ai voulu qu'un nom habillé de quelque lustre fût traîné sur les bancs d'une école de correction ; j'ai fait inscrire sous le nom de Pierre Buffière ce monsieur qui a recalcitré, pleuré, ratiociné en pure perte ; et je lui ai dit de gagner mon nom, que je ne lui rendrait qu'à bon escient." —June 8, 1764, to the *bailli*. Mém., I. 276.

have burned an indelible mark on his, the father's, forehead.

In 1767, Pierre Buffière was put into the army. From this time the feud between father and son rapidly sinks into darker and darker depths. The son now comes in for a steadily and fast increasing share of real guilt, but his guilt is always outrun by the father's unreasonable, unjust, and despotic paternalism.

Time does not allow me to sketch even with a few words all the phases of the bitter contest. I can only with the utmost brevity direct the attention to some facts, which are indispensable to the correct understanding of the times and of the bearing which Mirabeau's ante-revolutionary career had upon the course of the revolution.

Debts, contracted at the gambling table and in all sorts of other indulgences of a more or less reprehensible character, and an indiscreet and impure love affair, caused his father to resume the idea I just alluded to. He thought of sending the son to the Dutch colonies, *because* their mephitic climate rendered it rather more than likely that he would never return from them.[1] Many a year

---

[1] That the "because" is fully justified, the following sentences from a letter of the much kindlier *bailli* amply

later Mirabeau wrote from his terrible dungeon in Vincennes to his father: "You have confessed to me in one of your letters, that from the time of my imprisonment on the island Rhé you have been on the point of sending me to the Dutch colonies. The word has made a deep impression upon me and influenced in a high degree my after-life. . . . What had I done at the age of eighteen years, that you could conceive such an idea, which makes me tremble even now, when I am buried alive? . . . I had made love."[1] Why do Loménie and Stern not quote this letter? It seems to me that it *must* be quoted, if one is to judge fairly.

The project was abandoned in favor of a milder means, which the *ancien régime* offered to persons of high standing and influence to rid themselves of people who were in their way, the so-called *lettres de cachet*. The person whose name a complacent minister entered upon the formulary[2] was arrested

proves: "Ask yourself, whether the excesses of this miserable fellow do not deserve that he should be forever cast out of society; in this case it would be best, as you say, to send him to the Dutch colonies. One would be sure to see never again appear on the horizon a wretch, who is born to cause grief to his neighbors and be the shame of his family."

[1] Lettres de Vincennes, I. 196.
[2] Sometimes they were even given *in blanco*.

in the name of the king and disappeared, without trial or judgment, in some state prison for as long a time as his persecutor chose to keep him caged. By this handy means the marquis now began to drag his son from prison to prison, in his " quality of natural tribunal," as he said.[1]

Loménie lays considerable stress upon the fact that once or twice Mirabeau seems to have been rather satisfied with thus being taken care of, because he was thereby protected from his creditors. The marquis, however, gains but little by that. As to his son he appears, in regard to this particular instance, in a better light than before this fact was unearthed, but from the other side a new shadow falls upon him. Where did this fanatic of duty find the moral justification to prevent the creditors from getting their due by thus putting their debtor "under the hand of the king," as the phrase ran?[2]

---

[1] The expression occurs in a very characteristic sentence, which makes one look aghast at this "Friend of Men," who was so sure that he had never harmed any one: "J'ai fait justice en qualité de tribunal naturel et domestique, et verrais sans remords, la mère sur les tréteaux, le fils à la Grève, et n'en irait pas moins la tête levée, et le sein découvert."— June 20, 1779, to the *bailli*. Mém., II. 314.

[2] He says quite naïvely: "Il vaut mieux qu'il soit mon prisonier que celui de ses créanciers." It is true, Mirabeau's revenues were to be applied to paying off his debts, but this, as he figured out, would keep him twenty-seven years in

It certainly could not be derived from any paragraph in his catechism. It is a most genuine piece of the code of the *ancien régime*.

For a number of years Mirabeau's debts constituted his principal wrong. He was one of those men who would somehow manage to get into debt even on a desert island and with Robinson's lump of gold for a pillow. But he would have had no opportunity to run up in the briefest time an account of over 200,000 francs, if he had not closely followed the father's bad example in choosing a wife. Miss Marignane was also an heiress, but—though bearing no resemblance to the *née* Miss Vassan—in almost every other respect pretty much the reverse of what a sensible man must wish his wife to be. Mirabeau would certainly never have thought of offering her his hand, if she had not been an heiress. His main reasons for wooing her seem, however, to have been the longing to become more independent of his father and a freak of petty vanity; he was tickled by the sensation it would cause that, in spite of his ugliness, the much

prison. Besides, though it was an exaggeration that, as he asserted, "pour aider à cette liquidation mon père touche bien mes revenus, mais ne paye rien," yet the father laid himself open to very grave reproaches in this respect.—See Mirabeau's Memoir of Apr. 16. 1776. Stern, I. 306, 307.

coveted prize was carried off by him. He did not even scruple to force the hand of the girl by gravely compromising her. But when she was his wife, he was only too gallant a knight. She was one of those women whose whole existence is comprised in sipping the cup of pleasure. She is, so to speak, all outside without any inside at all. If you want to get at her intellectual life, you must listen to her merry laugh about nothing at the picnic parties and the animated recitation of her part on the amateur stage, on which she is quite a star; and to find her heart, you must go to the milliner's and jeweler's shop.[1] To them and to the caterers Mirabeau carried the bulk of the money[2] he borrowed from the usurers. She had eaten up with her frivolities most of the money, for the squandering of which he had to pine his youth

[1] The *bailli* calls her " la plus sotte et la plus bégueule de son sexe." In another letter he says of her : " Elle s'est accoutumée à être le coryphée d'une société très-bruyante, qui passe du concert à la comédie, de là au bal, de là aux quatre points cardinaux, sur la plus petite apparence de fête ; elle est la divinité de tout ce monde, et tient à son piédestal."—Mém., III. 336, 333.

[2] The *bailli* writes : " Ce que j'ai vu de relatif aux dettes de ton fils est, pour les trois quarts au moins, pour présens faits à sa femme. Qui plus est il y en a pour le beau-père." The father admits the truth of the assertion : " La plus grande partie des créances valables est en fourniture d'utilité féminine."—Mém., III. 346.

away in prison. And that was not all she had to answer for. She too had enjoyed all the advantages of good example, and she profited as much by it as Mirabeau. Her grandmother and her mother were separated from their husbands, and very soon she gave Mirabeau the right to bid her leave his house forever. He forgave her the adultery, of which she stood convicted by her own confession, and he never told any one of her shame, until he thought that by revealing his magnanimity he could induce the courts to compel her to rejoin him. She thanked him for his generosity by telling him that he was a fool, when he implored and commanded her to join him in his place of detention, in order to stand between him and the temptation which threatened to close the gulf over him by pushing him from guilt into crime. Aye, Mirabeau sinned much, but he was infinitely more sinned against.[1]

In Pontarlier, while he was officially a prisoner at Fort Joux, he and Sophie, the wife of President Monnier, fell in love with each other. Sophie was

---

[1] "Bref, sa femme a eu plus de torts que lui, car, pendant ses souffrances, elle était sur les tréteaux ; et, à dire vrai, Honoré, quoique bien coupable, a été encore plus malheureux."—The *bailli* to the marquis. Dec. 3, 1772. Mém., III. 344.

twenty-four and her husband seventy years old. She had married him because her parents wanted her to, and he had married her principally to spite a daughter from his first wife, who had married against his will. There were people who thought the old bigot had in truth no objection to somebody else's helping him to beget a son, in order not to let his fortune go to that daughter. Intellectual affinity had little to do with the love of the two young people, though an unruly and exuberant imagination was a trait common to both. The animal senses were the main source of their mutual passion. Indulgence did not quench the fire but fanned it. The scandal after a while became of such a character, that no amount of complacency on the part of the authorities could any longer render it compatible with Mirabeau's official status as prisoner. He fled, probably breaking his word of honor, though he asserts that he had been released from his promise. The father, more ready to spend money to punish than to help the son, hired some detectives from the government to hunt him down. He always gave them the slip—at least once at the eminent risk of his life. At last he recrossed the frontier, was joined by Sophie, and escaped with her to Holland. A suit was instituted against them. She was sentenced to confinement for life in a convent, he to death. His picture was nailed to the gallows. That they had rendered themselves amenable to the penal law, is indisputable. This sentence, however, was a judicial outrage. According to the moral code of the social classes, to which they belonged, they were — as the *bailli* afterwards maintained — hardly guilty of more than a petty offence. In the eyes of these circles their real crime consisted not in what they had done, but in the "crying publicity" of their wickedness.[1]

The fugitives worried but little about the sentence, for they deemed themselves perfectly safe. They might have been, if Mirabeau had not provoked his father afresh. The marquis thought that he was forever rid of him, and he was glad of it. He was honestly desirous of being allowed to

[1] "Fallait-il . . . que d'un fait très-vulgaire on fît une monstruosité sans exemple et de la morale, et de la théorie, et du dogme?"—"Qui, dans cette infâme Babylone (Paris) où tous les scandales sur tel sujet sont sondés, cicatrisés, consolidés n'est pas, de fait ou de volonté, de ce qu'il a eu de répréhensible essentiellement, dans la conduite de l'*infaillible* (Mirabeau)? Qu'il y ait mis plus d'éclat, cela est vrai; mais le fond des choses est le même; mais, adultère, rapt, séduction, en le supposant coupable des trois, et il ne l'est que d'un, c'est l'histoire de tous ou presque tous; il n'y a que la publicité bruyante de plus."—Mém., III. 253, 254.

consider him henceforth as simply non-existing. The suit of his wife against him frustrated the realization of this hope. The mother induced the son to champion her cause before public opinion and the court. He wrote and published a memoir against his father, brimful of concentrated venom. It was the meanest and vilest deed of his life. Though he maintained that his father had no longer any moral claim upon him,[1] he afterwards declared in a letter, which cannot possibly have been written for effect, that he regretted this act "with tears of blood."

Before Mirabeau's flight from Dijon, his father, supported by other relatives, had already requested the minister Malesherbes to have him locked up in Pierre-en-Cise for so long a time as he, the father, should deem fit, and not to allow him any communication whatever with the outer world.[2]

---

[1] "Mon père a outre-passé envers moi les droits d'un homme quelconque sur un autre homme, et par conséquent d'un père sur son fils, et ainsi brise la chaîne de mes devoirs envers lui." The oppressed has the duty to resist the oppressor, and "dans nos pays esclaves, on ne peut arrêter le crédit dans sa marche inique et tortueuse, qu'en suscitant contre lui l'opinion publique."—May 12, 1779, to Boucher. Mém., IV. 49. It is interesting that Mirabeau partly excuses himself by "ma maudite facilité à écrire."

[2] The naïve frankness with which he enunciates his paternalistic notions in this memoir is fairly startling: "S'il

Now he was determined not to rest ere he had succeeded in making an end of it in this way. Not just indignation alone prompted him to this resolution. Nothing was to be left undone to deprive his wife of the aid of this powerful pen, for the thought that he might lose the suit, was utterly unbearable to him.

The States-General, against their wont, consented to the extradition.[1] On June 7, 1777, the

(Mirabeau) doit l'être (*i. e.*, free) encore, je m'en lave les mains et devant Dieu et devant les hommes, mais je mets sur la conscience du ministre tous les délits qui en résulteront ... quand l'autorité tutélaire et souveraine se refuse à appuyer l'autorité domestique, reconnue impartiale et équitable, elle sait sans doute, où prendre les ressorts, propres à veiller sur la tête de chaque individu en particulier. Je m'y résigne donc, mais elle ne pourra refuser un jour à ma vieillesse, qui viendra lui demander compte de la prostitution d'un nom, qui m'avait été transmis sans tache et que j'avais tâché de conservé tel, son secours pour le dérober du moins à la flétrissure, portés par les lois."—Stern, I. 302, 303. The refusal of the government to give him possession of the trunks of the son, after imprisoning him at his demand in the Donjon, fills him with the deepest indignation. "Il faut qu'on nous ait outrecuidamment oubliés, nous et nos ascendans. pour que, quand nous enfermons notre propre géniture, on nous marchande et nous rogne notre autorité."
—Mém., II. 284, 285.

[1] Fr. Kapp (*Soldatenhandel deutscher Fürsten nach America*) is of opinion that the Landgrave of Hessia, whom Mirabeau had denounced in a pamphlet for selling his subjects to the English to help them subdue the rebellious Americans, influenced them. From the Donjon Mirabeau

gates of the Donjon de Vincennes closed upon Mirabeau. His father intended that they should never again open for him. " Besides the official authorities," he wrote to the *bailli*, " I alone want to know his place of confinement; after my death it shall be revealed to my successor by a sealed letter." And that to a son, of whom he himself declared again and again, that at bottom his heart was good, and that perhaps not a man could be found in France less capable of a premeditated wickedness.[1] Yes, indeed, a heart that was at bottom good. When at last after three and a half years he was allowed to re-enter life on trial, the tears rushed from his eyes when he saw a portrait of his father, and from his trembling lips fell but two words, which in their simplicity are the most

repeatedly and urgently requested to be allowed to join the French army in America.—Lettres de Vincennes, I. 424 ; III. 369. Lettres de cachet, I. 284.

[1] " Il a une sensibilité turbulente, qui le rend bon et non mauvais. Mais, au fond, il a nulle bonté, pas même pour lui-même, qu'il tracasse et qu'il traite comme un chien et comme un cheval : du reste, peut-être a-t-il besoin, de se tarabuster ainsi, car son exubérance sanguine l'étoufferait ; et, en vérité, soyons justes, il y a bien du physique dans ses écarts."—" Au fond, cet homme, qui n'a que l'escrime de satan, mais non sa griffe, n'a pas de méchanceté pour liards; mais il a des trésors d'enfance et de folie."—" Au fond, c'était peut-être l'homme du royaume le plus incapable d'une méchanceté réfléchie."—Mém., III. 270, 255, 174.

beautiful monument which he has erected to himself as a man: "Poor father!" And this "poor father," though his heart had somewhat softened towards the son, was not primarily induced by its appeals to unlock the prison door.[1] He wanted to make use of his supposed influence upon the mother, he wished to effect a reconciliation between Mirabeau and his wife, because during his imprisonment his only legitimate son had died and the marquis craved with all the intensity of his ardent heart to see the race continued in the male line, and above all he had become seriously afraid that his son would obtain his release without and against him, if he did not grant it.[2] These were

[1] The father himself admits that there was no acting in this scene. "Du Saillant, qui a mis dehors son beau-frère, en est fort content à tous égards, lui qui ne s'enthousiasme guère ; il s'attendait à trouver du théatral et du pathos, il a trouvé un homme fort touché, fort repentant, fort soumis, et surtout pénétré, à sa furieuse mode, pour son père et sa famille ; en même temps gaillard et leste pour tout autre. . . . Voyant mon portrait, il fut extrêmement touché, et il fondit en larme ne disant que *pauvre père!*"—Dec. 20, 1780, to the *bailli*. Mém., III. 123. Some weeks before Mirabeau had written in a letter, which could not possibly come to the knowledge of his family or any person of influence : "Si je puis arracher une larme de lui, me voilà payé de tout ce que son despotisme m'a fait perdre et souffrir."—Mém., II. 321.

[2] "Si je n'eusse lâché mon fils, mes ennemis me l'allaient arracher et tous m'auraient jeté la pierre."—Febr. 16, 1781.

the determining reasons of the marquis. He had not and never did become conscious of having to reproach himself in the least in regard to this arbitrary imprisonment of forty-two months.[1] On the contrary, he was satisfied that he had done the son a very good turn by it. And before he pushed back the bolt, he had secured from the government the right to put him again, at any moment, behind lock and key, without having to render any account to anybody.[2] The *bailli* preaches in vain, that a man of thirty-three years is too old to be

---

"Compte qu'Honoré, peu s'en faut, en mesure de sortir de Vincennes, sans nous."—Mem., II. 370. Mirabeau had threatened to move heaven and earth. "D'être remis, soit aux juges ordinaires, soit à des commissaires . . . pour que mon procès, instruit et jugé, m'apprenne enfin pourquoi, depuis sept ans je suis privé de la liberté."—See Lettres de Vincennes, IV. 198, *sq.*

[1] "Quarante-deux mois dans un lieu où l'on n'a, pour toute compagnie dans des voutes gothiques et lugubres, que les hurlemens nocturnes des souterrains et autres voisinages, sont une médicine qui doit renouveler une tête; il faut du malheur à l'homme; mais nous ne sommes pas à bout, et je garantirai sa femme de son enthousiasme, comme je l'ai fait de ses folies; le tout pour l'acquit de mon devoir." —Mém., III. 126. He says now of him: "C'est un homme fait, qui se contient, et qui est même imposant, malgré cette extrême vivacité dont il est néanmoins le maître . . . il a doublé d'esprit. . . . Il voit comme un aigle."—Mém., III. 151.

[2] Mirabeau wrote Sept. 29, 1782, in regard to this to the minister Vergennes: "Mais observez, M. le comte, que par la nature de l'ordre du Roi qui me grève, je peux sans

kept in leading strings.[1] The marquis persists in his old doctrine, that it is his duty to guide, and the son's duty to obey.[2]

I cannot enter upon the story of Mirabeau's sufferings at the Donjon. Only one statement must be made. He probably would have succumbed to them—physically, mentally, and morally —if it had not been for the manifold and great kindnesses done him by his jailers, partly in flagrant violation of the prison rules. This too is a very characteristic trait of the *ancien régime*. The government—though an uncommonly good-natured king sits on the throne and the ministers are upright and kindly men—drives a Juggernaut

aucune information nouvelle, sans même aucune imputation, et au premier signe de mon père y (any state prison) rentrer. Cet ordre, j'ose le dire, est inconcevable, est inouï. Le Roi n'a ni dû, ni pû se départir de ses droits de protection et de juridiction sur moi, me déclarer en quelque sorte hors de l'empire de la loi et de sa volonté."—Stern, I. 313.

[1] " Prends garde, d'ailleurs, que la manière de ne réussir à rien, c'est se vouloir penser pour les autres, et de vouloir mener selon son propre goût, non suivant le leur."—Aug. 3, 1781. "Si, à trente-trois ans, on ne peut laisser aller ton fils, avec les punitions qu'il a essuyées, tu entreprends de sécher la rivière à la façon des Danaïdes."—Sept. 4, 1781. Mém., III. 170.

[2] " Quand il se conduit bien et obéit, je dois aussi le conduire. . . . Tout cela n'est pas affaire de choix et de volonté, mais de devoir."—July 21, 1781. Mém., III. 171.

car over the subjects, and its lower organs clandestinely pile pillows over the victims to save them from being completely crushed.

Dark enough are the details of this story of grief, but though they were ten times darker, from the historian's point of view they would weigh but little in the scales compared to the fact in itself, that a man is kept in prison three years and a half not only without trial and judgment, but without any legal charge whatever being brought against him. Already in the memoir replying to the father's petition to have him incarcerated for an indefinite time at Pierre-en-Cise, Mirabeau had written: "If I deserve to be punished, let it be legally established and let me be legally punished."[1] From his cell in the Donjon he again and again reiterated this demand with increasing insistence. Even according to the twisted logic of the *ancien régime* it was unanswerable. According to the ethics of the *ancien réigme*, however, there was not the slightest objection to its being simply ignored. But the times were past when it could be ignored with impunity. Some years later, in a letter to the minister Montmorin, Mirabeau warned the government to

[1] Stern, I. 306.

beware "of that terrible malady of ministers, that they can never make up their minds to give to-day what will inevitably be wrenched from them to-morrow."[1] He spoke advisedly and with authority, that is to say, not as a theorist, but as a man of action, who had made it the one task of his life to bring about the fulfilment of the prophetic warning. He had commenced working at it almost from the moment the government of the *ancien régime* had consented to become his father's willing handmaid in making him the most striking object lesson of the incalculable blessings of despotic paternalism. With glowing passion and terrific energy he had devoted himself ever more and more to this task, and his pen had become a dreaded power in the state. The father and the ministers of the crown had been unwittingly engaged in a hot contest, as to who could do the most and the best towards training the most implacable and the most formidable enemy of the existing order of things.

Mirabeau had entered the lists with the "Essay on Despotism."[2] As a literary production it was,

---

[1] Apr. 18, 1788. Mém., IV. 483.
[2] Written 1772 in Manosque.
[3] See Lettres de Vincennes, II. 444.

in his own opinion, worth but little.³ He wanted it principally to be considered "as a profession of faith as a citizen."¹ Judged as such it throws a strange sidelight upon the father, who persisted in consigning again and again this youth to the "dunghill." He preaches in it with equal emphasis the doctrine of popular sovereignty in its most rigorous form,² and the wisdom of obviating despotism by daring to tell the truth to the monarchs, proving to them that their own interest requires the limitation of their authority, for "in augmenting their authority, they diminish their power:" "a prince who arrogates to himself all authority, loses it all."³ Distinctly, though naturally still in a somewhat inchoate state, this first youthful production already reveals the uncompromising revolutionist, as well as the conservative monarchical statesman.

The father was of opinion, that "one must be insane to write such things when one is in the bonds of a *lettre de cachet.*" The son gloried in it, that he had dared to "thunder against despotism," while he was himself weighed down by it.⁴ To increase the weight of his chains was the surest

---

[1] Oct. 22, 1776, to Marc-Michel Rey.—Mém., IV. 5.
[2] Ib., 32, 102, 274; edition of 1775. [3] Ib., 81, 95. [4] Ib., IV. 6.

means to make him thunder all the louder. In the Donjon he wrote a larger work, " On the *Lettres de Cachet* and the State Prisons." [1] The judgment which he passed upon this effort contrasted sharply with his criticism upon the " Essay on Despotism." In his cell he penned the proud words: "It will not die."[2] It was, indeed, sure not to die, ere the *lettres de cachet* were dead and buried beyond resurrection, a new age closing the tomb for all time to come. It was more than a book: it was a political deed, for it contained, as he said, "what no one else either would have dared to say, or could have said."[3] It was not written merely with ink, but also with his heart's blood. The prisoner sat in judgment upon the *ancien régime*, and under his terrible arraignment the royal palace at Versailles shook, as if the wave of an earthquake had passed under it. He had not become a convert to the doctrine, that one ought to thunder against despotism only when one is well out of harm's way. " My work on the state prisons," he writes to the father, " is not without some merit, for my mind emboldened by persecution, has elevated my genius repressed by

[1] 1778; published 1782.
[2] Lettres de Vincennes, III. 63.   [3] Ib., IV. 323.

suffering."[1] "Free or not, to my last breath I shall contend for the rights of mankind," he announced in the book itself—he was in dead earnest about it—and it was the truth that persecution only emboldened him. Had his father forgotten that even as a child he had known no fear? The courage of the man was not only boundless, but of an imposing and overpowering fierceness. "As many as you are, you will never succeed in making me tremble," he wrote to his sister, when he had voluntarily returned to prison in Pontarlier, in order to put his head again firmly upon his shoulders by compelling the court to revoke its sentence against him and Sophie.[2] "The sight of the scaffold opposite my window would not induce me to accept propositions in prison"[3] —thus he declined a proposed compromise. He was the genuine grandson of old Jean Antoine, who delighted in running in front of a column of assault and in baring his bosom on a breach.

And what an excellent schooling had his adversaries and persecutors managed to provide for him for the arena, in which soon the decisive contests

[1] Lettres de Vincennes, II. 222.
[2] Lettres inédites de Mirabeau à Vitry, 196; Mém., III. 256.
[3] Mém., III. 260.

of the age were to take place. He was certainly a born orator, but even of the born orator the old saying holds good, that practice makes the master. And not only his numerous memoirs addressed to the ministers and to the court, but also his countless private letters pleading his cause, were so many oratorical efforts, though they were only written and never spoken. The judges at Pontarlier and Aix had a story to tell about what he had profited by this practice. There he cowed and terrorized them, and here—pleading for an order of the court compelling his wife to rejoin him—in a speech of five hours he almost literally crushed the defendant's attorney, and he the celebrated Portalis. His father wrote about this scene: " His opponent, whom they had to carry fainting and shattered (*foudroyé*) out of the room, has not been able to leave his bed since the terrible five-hours' pleading, in which he was crushed;" and, " Imagine the triumph of this rope-dancer; on the day of the great spectacle the intoxicated crowd, although the guard had been trebled, occupied and smashed doors, barriers, windows, everything; even on the roofs they sat, to see him at least, if they could not hear him; and it is a pity that they did not all hear him, for he has spoken so much, howled so much, roared so much, that the mane of the lion was white with froth and the perspiration dripped from it." [1] And this man had vowed hatred and persecution unto death to the despotism of the *ancien régime*.

Even two hours more would not afford me sufficient time for the briefest sketch of his warfare against it and his checkered career during the next seven years, till the meeting of the States-General ushers in a new era of the history of Europe. There is many a dark page in them, but the light also grows ever more intense. The numerous writings of this period, judged from the literary point of view, can lay no claim to being masterpieces. How could they be? "It seems to be my fatal destiny," he says, "that I am always compelled to do everything in twenty-four hours." [2] But they are almost all, like the "Essay on Despotism," professions of faith, and more or less, like the "Lettres de Cachet," not merely books and pamphlets, but political deeds.

With breathless rapidity he strikes blow upon blow, but—the dust and the mould of many state prisons lie thick upon his garments and their

[1] Mém., III. 407, 408.
[2] Febr. 10, 1789, to M. de Comps. Mém., V. 262.

hem is saturated with filth. What of that? Did the splinters not fly, wherever he struck, just the same as if the arm that smote had been as pure as it was strong? Sure enough, they did. And still—what of that, indeed! In the strict sense of the word it was a fearful calamity to France, and thereby to Europe. With that baby of repulsive ugliness the Fates had entrusted to the "Friend of Men" the most precious life in France. Ah, if he had, as he said of his son, "seen like an eagle," if he had but had something of the prophetic gift of this miscreant! The *ancien régime* had bred in his heart and in his head his perverse paternalistic notions, and by making the most of the possibilities afforded to him by the *ancien régime* in driving to ruthless excess their application, he had rendered impossible the realization of this baby's grand possibilities. But for his mad conception of duty it could never have come to this, that in the grandest political era of France, her greatest political genius would have to say, and the bitter word hold good to the last day of his life, nay beyond the gates of death: "How strange this destiny of mine, always to be the promoter of a revolution, and always between a dunghill and a palace." [1]

[1] Lettres à Mauvillon, 449.

LECTURE VI.

The States-General.

I STATED in a former lecture the negative purport of the convocation of the States-General: the government announced that the *ancien régime* had to go into liquidation and made a formal assignment. Positively it settled absolutely nothing, except that France was to enter upon a new chapter of her history. In itself it neither determined nor even indicated anything whatever in regard to the character the contents of this chapter were to bear. The States-General were themselves a piece[1] of the *ancien régime* and a

---

[1] As they were convened only sixteen times it is in a sense hardly justified to call them an institution. The first convocation took place in 1302 and was occasioned by the contentions of Philippe le Bel with Pope Boniface VIII. Pasquier, however, contends that it is not correct to call this assembly States General. According to him these were convened for the first time in 1314.—Recherches de la France, livre II, chap. VII; Archives Parlem., I. 49. Some author-

thoroughly genuine one, though when the *ancien régime* degenerated into royal absolutism, the government of course condemned it to become and remain a dead historical reminiscence; for to allow the representatives of the three orders any real power was incompatible with absolutism, and the surest way not to let them aspire to any real power was not to convene them at all. But the government deemed it only prudent not to run any risk on this head. It was not to be inferred from their not being convened, that they could rightfully claim any power, if they were convoked. When an opportunity offered itself, the government took good care to warn the people emphatically against being betrayed into such an inadmissible notion. Replying to an *arrêt* of the Parliament of Paris of January 14, 1719, Guillaume de Lamoignon said : " We recognize in France no other sovereign than the king. His authority makes the laws: as the king wills, thus wills the law. To the States-General no way is open but that of remonstrance and very humble supplication. The king pays heed to their griev-

---

ities count as many as twenty meetings of the States-General: 1302, 1315, 1321, 1328, 1355, 1356, 1357, 1358, 1359, 1369, 1380, 4681, 1483, 1558, 1560, 1561, 1576, 1588, 1614, 1789.

ances and requests according to the rules of his wisdom and justice." [1]

If the government now proposed to adhere to and maintain this old doctrine, it virtually declared : Whereas I have been compelled to announce to the nation that the *ancien régime* is completely and irretrievably broken down, I have summoned the States-General to assist me, as they will be in duty bound, not in attempting to restore political vitality to the kingdom, but to see to it that it remain, to the dishonor and ruin of the people, a pitiable and repellent labyrinth of unrepairable ruins. Of such a palpable absurdity the government was not guilty. It set out by formally assigning them a very different task. But it neither clearly defined and circumscribed

[1] As late as 1776, the Parliament of Paris emphatically endorsed this doctrine. In an *arrêté* of March 20 of that year, it declared : "Il résulte des anciennes maximes nationales, attestées à chaque page de notre histoire, qu'au roi seul appartient le droit de convoquer les Etats Généraux ; que *lui seul* doit juger si cette convocation est *utile* et *nécessaire ;* qu'il n'a besoin d'aucun pouvoir extraordinaire pour l'administration de son royaume ; qu'un roi de France ne pourrait trouver dans les représentations des trois ordres de l'Etat qu'un *Conseil plus étendu*, composé des membres choisis d'une famille dont il est le chef, et qu'il serait toujours l'arbitre suprême de leurs représentations ou de leurs doléances."
—Quoted by Cassagnac, Histoire des Causes de la Révolution française, II. 209.

this task, nor did it with any precision state what the character and extent of authority were to be, with which it intended to consider them invested for the purpose of accomplishing this task. That the people did not receive definite information on these points was bad enough. But it was infinitely worse, that the government was very far from knowing its own mind in regard to any of them. To such a degree was it unaware of the tremendous importance of having these preliminary questions authoritatively decided before the meeting of the States-General, that it had manifestly not even bestowed any serious consideration upon them. One thing only shone forth in but too great clearness from the haze in which it moved: like the court it wanted the new with the old, but not the new in place of the old.

The king's letter of January 24, 1789, to the governors in regard to the convocation of the States-General,[1] ordered, that the deputies should be "furnished with instructions and general and sufficient powers to propose, urge, advise, and approve everything that may concern the needs of the state, the reform of abuses, the establishment of a fixed and lasting order in all the

[1] Archives Parlementaires, I. 611.

branches of administration, the general prosperity of our kingdom, and the welfare of all and every one of our subjects." It certainly did not require any forced interpretation to see in this more than ordinary legislative functions. Still it was not directly said that the States-General were to be a constituent assembly — to devise a constitution for France. The wording was sufficiently vague to admit of honest differences of opinion covering the whole ground between yes and no. When it became apparent that the overwhelming majority of the people understood, in accordance with the law laid down by the stern facts of the situation, that the States-General were also to act as a constituent assembly, the government did not intimate that it had been misunderstood. Yet even ordinary legislative powers were not conceded to them in an incontestable manner by the king's letter. In this respect too the fence had seemed the most advisable seat to the government. On the one hand, the king bound himself "to maintain and have executed whatever should be *concerted*" between him and them, and on the other, he, in the very same sentence, only promised "to ask and hear *favorably* their *advice* about all that can be of interest to the welfare of our people, and to *provide* in regard to their grievances and propositions."

Thus the government blew hot and cold with the same breath, leaving everything undetermined as to the position it would ultimately take and assuming no binding obligation whatever. But however fearful the possibilities with which this indecision was fraught, could the government do otherwise so long as another preliminary question was not settled? Whether the States-General were merely to give advice or to be clad with more or less real authority, was it to be presumed that they themselves would ever agree as to what ought to be done? Unless an age of miracles dawned for France, this was next to impossible, if these States-General were to be the States-General of old. The reason is simply that the historical States-General were not a national representation, but the representation of three orders. Two of these were invested with privileges, the abolishment of most of which was an absolute prerequisite of the regeneration of the body politic. Was it likely that they would voluntarily relinquish them to the extent imperatively demanded by the public interest? If they did not, nothing could be attained, for as the vote was taken by orders, they could in every single question outvote the third by two to one. Even if, from patriotism or an enlightened view of its own interests, one of them were to join the third, it would avail but little, for in questions concerning the whole, each had a veto upon the two others. Therefore, if the States-General of 1789 were to be what the States-General of former centuries had been, their convocation was almost tantamount to decreeing that this last attempt at setting the commonwealth again on its feet must be a failure. Nay, it would have resulted of necessity in worse than a mere failure. Mirabeau did not draw upon his imagination, when on the 15th of June he warned the assembled deputies of the third order: "I need not color this slight sketch to demonstrate that the division of the orders, the veto of the orders, the arguing and deliberating by orders, would be a truly sublime invention to fix constitutionally egoism in the priesthood, pride in the patriciate, baseness in the people, discord between all interests, corruption in all the classes composing the great family, cupidity in all minds, insignificance of the nation, tutelage of the prince, despotism of the ministers."[1]

[1] Œuvres, I. 221.

That was the true scope of the question. Though it was well known that the two upper orders were prepared to consent to a curtailment of the pecuniary advantages they were now enjoying, nobody could guarantee that they would be willing to go far enough; and to run any risk on this head would have been a dereliction of duty on the part of the representatives of the third order towards their constituents. If any of them did not see this before repairing to Versailles, Necker did his best to unseal their eyes the very first day. His greeting to the States-General contained the declaration, that "a system of compensation or indemnity" must be provided for, in case the noble estates [1] were to be deprived of their exemption from taxation. The first word of the government an assurance, that it would use padded velvet gloves in handling the privileges! Could that be calculated to stimulate the liberality of the privileged orders? But even if they had unanimously promised in writing to make the most liberal concessions, the third estate would not have been satisfied, and justly so. They did

---

[1] Not estates of noblemen. The exemptions, as I have mentioned before, attached to the estate and not to the owner. A fief owned by a *bourgeois* was free, and a *roturier* estate owned by a nobleman had to pay.

not request concessions; they demanded as an incontestable right the unconditional recognition of the principle of equality. As to this very question of principle, however, the privileged orders put their feet down as squarely and firmly as the third estate.[1] They were willing to assume a larger share of the public burdens, but as a concession and without renouncing their character as privileged orders. We meet with the formal declaration, that the offer is due only to "respect for the monarch and love for his person," and that therefore the tax shall be distinguished by name as the "*taille noble*" and conceded only for a limited period. And La Fare, the bishop of

[1] "En parlant pour la noblesse, les princes de votre sang parlent pour eux-mêmes; ils ne peuvent oublier qu'ils forment partie du corps de la noblesse, qu'ils n'en doivent point être distingués; que leur premier titre est d'être gentilshommes... Que le tiers-état cesse donc d'attaquer les droits des deux premiers ordres; droits qui, non moins anciens que la monarchie, doivent être aussi inaltérables que sa constitution; qu'il se borne à solliciter la diminution des impôts dont il peut être surchargé; alors les deux premiers ordres, reconnaissant dans le troisième des citoyens qui leur sont chers, pourront, par la générosité de leurs sentiments (!), renoncer aux prérogatives qui ont pour objet un intérêt pécuniaire, et consentir à supporter dans la plus parfaite égalité les charges publiques."—Mémoire présenté au roi par monseigneur comte d'Artois, M. le prince de Condé, M. le duc de Bourbon, M. le duc d'Enghien et M. le prince de Conti. Archives Parlem., I. 488.

Nancy, in the sermon preached at the opening of the States-General, emphatically asserted: " The renunciation of exemptions is a voluntary sacrifice which nobody has a right to demand" (*exiger*).[1]

If the States-General deliberated and voted by orders, the principle underlying this claim applied to everything. In other words: to the majority of each of the three orders was conceded as well the power as the right to thwart the saving of the country. A principle was involved in the question, and on this principle depended, legally and practically, everything. If the government conceded the principle to the privileged orders, because what they claimed had been 175 years ago the law of the land, it deliberately abandoned everything to chance. To say that it was bound to do so, was on its face an utter absurdity, unless it was admitted that there was a possibility of saving France by screwing her back into the conditions of two centuries ago. If the privileged orders would not go to that length, they had no answer to two simple propositions: it is self-stultification to assert, that the government is precluded from summoning a representation of the three estates constituting the nation to its assistance in

[1] Œuvres, I. 174.

devising ways and means for saving the country, unless it be exactly the same kind of representation, which even six generations ago proved to be no longer in accordance with the requirements of the times; and, even if it were true that historical precedent still constitutes law, though the institution of the States-General has practically not existed for almost two centuries, the country does not exist for the law—if the nation is pushed before the alternative of letting either the country or the law go by the board, the latter must go. The government did not assent to either of the two doctrines, nor did it set up one of its own. It chose to assume an absolutely negative attitude. Its principle and programme was to have neither principle nor programme.

What the outcome of the convocation of the States-General would be nobody could tell, but as to one thing all were agreed: to shelve them once more for an indefinite time would be impossible. We have heard that the Parliament in its resolutions of May 3, 1788, had declared it one of the fundamental laws of the realm, that they " be convened at stated intervals." Necker, however, was unquestionably right in saying, that to make in this sense a permanent institution of the old States-

General was "to order chaos"; but he was of opinion that a fusion of the three orders would be effected of itself by general consent, at first in regard to specific questions, and then gradually generalized.[1] He was satisfied that if one began to pray "good devil," one would smoothly drift into praying "good Lord." And he concluded that the surest way to achieve this desirable result was to set all the sails and let the helm take care of itself. To the third estate the double number of deputies was accorded,[2] but nothing was said about how the States-General were to deliberate and vote. If this was to be done by orders, the double number did not avail the third estate anything. Still in one respect the concession was far from being irrelevant; it raised the wind most

[1] Loménie, IV. 286.

[2] Mirabeau, in one of his letters to Cerutti, asserts: "Cette crainte (that it would not be done) n'était pas sans fondement, puisque M. Necker a longtemps hésité, puisque des décisions intérieures avaient décreté la proportion contraire, puisque, en un mot, les seules remontrances des gens d'affaires, des prêteurs d'argent, nous l'ont obtenue... Oui, c'est à la protection des banquiers que la nation doit la résolution d'un ministre auquel on a voulu dresser des autels."— Mémoires, V. 216. A considerable pressure was exercised upon the government by the threat that, in case the concession were refused, the third estate would elect and send to Versailles a much larger number of deputies even than it now demanded.—See Mémoires, VI. 13.

effectually. Surely, any political tyro might have foreseen that it would do so. There was, indeed, no more room for conjecture on this score, for the facts had already proved it in a most impressive way. After the convocation of the States-General had been decided upon, the Parliament of Paris had declared as to the question of the How, that it should be in the form observed in 1614. It thereby shattered at one blow all the popularity it had gained by its former contests with the government. The indignation was so great that it tried hard to explain away the unfortunate words, but the blunder was irremediable. It only added contempt to indignation. There was nobody to accord it even the bitter consolation of pity. Even from the good-natured king it could get nothing but the dry answer: "I have nothing to reply to my Parliament and its requests."

Here was a manifestation of the power of public opinion, which ought to have been fully appreciated by the man, who the year before had so sensibly commented upon the fact, that this mysterious power commanded even in the palace of the king. And now public opinion could bring its full force to bear upon the government, for the first step of the government after conceding the convocation of the States-General had been formally to invite[1] everybody to say whatever he happened to know about the obsolete institution.[2] Everybody is not only allowed, but even requested to swell the rising storm, by blowing into it with the full force of his lungs and from whatever direction he pleases. The invitation virtually granted the liberty of the press.[3] But it did more

[1] July 5, 1788.

[2] The government was not betrayed into this step by thoughtlessness. It was the culmination of Brienne's luminous idea to let the government take its revenge upon the privileged orders for raising the storm against it, by unfettering another storm against them. Louis XVI. adopted the suicidal advice. Wéber writes: "Il conçut dès ce moment l'idée de soulever le tiers contre les deux premiers ordres et d'en faire un rempart autour du Trône... Il employa dès lors toute son influence à susciter les prétentions du tiers contre l'ordre de la noblesse, et les principaux dépositaires de l'autorité du gouvernement eurent l'ordre de diriger les esprits vers ce mouvement, et de former une alliance défensive contre le peuple et la couronne."—Mém., I. 228, 238. This statement is corroborated by Sallier, Annales franç., 188, 189. Also Bouillé asserts that talented and zealous writers were sent for this purpose to the provinces.—Mém., I. 75. See also Mme. de Staël, Considérations, I. 127, and Barentin, Mém., 72. Cassagnac. II. 306, *sq.*

[3] The full import of this can be realized only by keeping in view what the law had been thus far in regard to the press. An *arrêt* of the *conseil* of March 22, 1785, had forbidden "à tous les journalistes à publier aucune lettre ou dissertation de quelque personne que ce fût, sur les matières de législation ou de jurisprudence, de même que de s'im-

than that. Though not in express words, yet with fearful distinctness did it proclaim the fact, that the government not only had no programme in summoning the States-General, but that it also did not propose to elaborate one now, to be submitted to them when they met. In this resolution Necker persisted.

Under the circumstances that was downright madness, and he could not even allege as an extenuation, that he blundered unwarned into what, as to its effects, amounted to an inexpiable political crime. Malouet told him: " You must not wait for the States-General to demand or command, you must make haste to offer all that the sound minds (*les bons esprits*) can, within reasonable limits, wish of authority, as well as of national rights." And he stated with the utmost plainness what this policy of no-policy really amounted to. " How could the ministers, ever since the end of 1788, reduce the king to a veritable suspension of his royal functions by the indecision which they allowed him to display in regard to the States-General? It was no longer the king that spoke, it was the attorney of the crown asking advice of the

miscer à interpreter les lois du royaume."—Manuel, Police dévoilée. Police de la librairie, I. 45.

whole world and seeming to tell everybody : What shall one do? What can I do? How far does one propose to retrench my authority? What will one leave me of it?"[1]

Did Malouet take too gloomy a view of the situation? Let us hear how it was judged by one greater than he.

I mentioned in a former lecture, that Mirabeau hailed with exultation the convocation of the Notables, because it must inevitably be followed by the convocation of the States-General. When afterwards Brienne promised to convene them within five years,[2] he (Mirabeau) wrote to a member of the Parliament: "The convocation of the States-General is to such a degree enjoined by necessity, so inevitable, that with or without the first minister, under Achilles or Thersites, it will unquestionably take place, and therefore but small thanks will be given to the government, at whatever time it may be resolved upon. But if it be put off for any length of time, that will be another cause of discontent, discredit, and ill-will."[3] Then, when the government has at last completely

[1] Quoted by Loménie, IV. 128.
[2] Nov. 19, 1787.
[3] Mémoires, IV. 463.

submitted to the inevitable,[1] his joy bursts forth with the impassioned ring of assured triumph. "With this step," he says in a letter to Mauvillon, "the nation advanced a whole century in twenty-four hours. Oh, my friend, you will see what this nation is able to do on the day which gives it a constitution, on the day when talent will also be a power."[2] Now, however, on the 8th of November, 1788, he writes: "The question which agitates us . . . involves the most important principles of the social order. It will decide the character which the revolution, that is in process with us, will assume; it will determine whether reason or prejudices, the general interest or private interests are to prevail in it, advance or force back our century. An extraordinary tribunal has been instituted to pass judgment on it. For the first time everybody is invited to speak and write. But this suit of the nation against the nation itself must be instituted and decided in less than two months! Such is the mastery of circumstances! Such is the forced march of events! France can no longer be governed except by the

---

[1] The promise to convene them on the 1st of May, 1789, was given on the 8th of August, 1788.

[2] Lettres à Mauvillon, 372.

States-General; we want to be assembled as a national body, but we do not know how to go about it."

Now, what did that signify: the character of the revolution, *i. e.*, everything depends on how this question is decided, and we do not know how to decide it? It meant nothing less than this: there is great danger that the glorious opportunity, which is offered, will be thrown away in preparing to improve it, and light may have pierced the darkness only to have us plunged into denser night. Before his penetrating eye this direful fact looms up in terrible distinctness, even before Necker has promulgated his programme of no-programme, and in sketching its ultimate consequences, he uses so full a brush, dipped into such flaming colors, that Malouet's dismal picture fades into utter insignificance. Brienne was dismissed on the 25th of August, and Mirabeau had already on the 19th written to the Count d'Antraigues: " This madman of an Archbishop is in a delirium. He would lead us into anarchy and democracy. If we do not look out, these people will republicanize us (*nous démonarchiseront*) and precipitate us into an abyss of calamities. We are going to have this charlatan Necker, the king of the populace (*canaille*). It alone has courage here, and if it should become master, it would finish by strangling everything under his direction."

Was this the wild talk of a man in a high fever? We have heard how public opinion had erected itself into a despotic fetish. According to public opinion, however, the outlook into the future presented a dazzling flood of light. One of the fruits of the philosophy of the 18th century was, that optimism had become epidemic. To illustrate how far the sanguine delusions went, it will suffice to mention, that even Turgot, the eminently practical statesman, ventured to promise the king, that an educational law, which he submitted to his approval, would change the people so completely within ten years, that henceforth only the dictates of " reason " would subject them to him and the laws. Barante says in his work on the French literature of the 18th century: "It was believed that civilization and enlightenment had killed all passions and tempered all characters." When the glad tidings sped through the country that the States-General had been convoked, the masses, too, were violently seized by the epidemic, but with them it at once assumed a peculiar character. De la Tour, the intendant of

Provence, reports even before the election: "The people have been persuaded that they will be relieved of all taxes, and that the first two orders will alone provide for all the needs of the state." And another time he writes: "The populace attacks indiscriminately priest, nobleman, bourgeois. The peasant continually announces that the destruction and pillage he perpetrates are in accordance with the will of the king." As late as December, 1790, Mirabeau speaks of "this kind of blind instinct which makes the people believe that for it the revolution consists in not having to pay anything."[1] These people could be made to believe anything. Small wonder! Gouverneur Morris painted pretty true to nature when he wrote from Paris on the 29th of April, 1789, to Washington: "The great mass of the common people have no religion but their priests, no law but their superiors, no morals but their interests. These are the creatures who, led by drunken curates, are now in the high road *à la liberté*, and the first use they make of it is to form insurrections everywhere for the want of bread."[2]

Yes, they could not only be made to believe

---

[1] Corresp., II. 421.
[2] J. Sparks, G. Morris, II. 69.

anything, but if what they had been made to believe was not fulfilled at once, they did not hesitate a moment to take the law into their own hands. Though they indiscriminately attacked the *bourgeois* also, as to the preliminary question, in regard to the States-General, they were fully agreed with the *bourgeoisie*. The intendant of Besançon writes on the 5th of December, 1788: "Last July the old Estates would have been hailed with delight and they would have met with little resistance. In the last five months, however, the minds have become enlightened, the different interests have been discussed, alliances have been concluded. You have not been informed, that in all classes of the third estate the fermentation has reached the climax, that one spark is sufficient to start a general conflagration. If the decision of the king should be favorable to the upper orders a general insurrection will break out in all parts of the province, 60,000 men will take up arms, and all the horrors of the Jacquerie will be repeated."

The king not deciding in favor of the upper orders, no general insurrection ensued. But there was nevertheless no lack of horrors. The king not deciding and not doing anything, France collapsed, as Taine says, into "spontaneous anarchy." That the government could not extricate her from this condition was manifest, for it was primarily due to the utter impotency and imbecility of the government; the popular passions did not rise to such a height, that they overflowed all the dikes, but all the dikes had crumbled away. Therefore, if chaos was again to be reduced into order, it had to be done by the States-General. But if the States-General were to do it, the *sine qua non* was, of course, that in regard to themselves everything be perfectly clear and settled. The government, however, not only refrained from deciding beforehand the all-important preliminary question, even when the States-General met no definite programme was laid before them—neither as to the How, nor as to the What.

At the solemn opening of the States-General on the 5th of May, 1789, the king said in his speech: "A general unrest, an overstrained desire for innovations, has taken possession of the minds and might end by confusing public opinion entirely, if one does not make haste to give it a hold by a combination of wise and moderate councils." But where were the wise and moderate councils? Not the slightest trace of any was to be found in the speech. "The minds," it said at another place, "are in agitation; but an assembly of representatives of the nation will, undoubtedly, hear only the voice of wisdom and prudence."[1] Will undoubtedly! Can a babe be more trustful! Sure enough—he tells the nation —it is an avalanche bearing straight down upon us. But why be scared? It is the business of these gentlemen to see to it, that its course be arrested ere any harm is done. That was virtually the abdication of the government.

While the king thus turns on his heel, saying: Now, gentlemen, you may try what you can accomplish in your wisdom-Necker had the effrontery to enlarge with the greatest self-complacency upon the self-evident untruth, that the king could very well have dispensed with the States-General. The reading of his speech—which he mostly left to a clerk—took three full hours. Though it contained, as Gouverneur Morris says, some fine passages, it was, upon the whole, in an eminent degree what it ought not to have been, and in no respect what it ought to have been. Mirabeau passed the following judgment upon it: "There are unquestionably some good details in this dis-

[1] Archives Parlementaires, VIII. 1.

course. But insupportable lengths, innumerable repetitions, trivialities pompously proclaimed, unintelligible things, not one principle, not one incontestable assertion, not one resource of the statesman, not even one great expedient of the financier, no plan of restoration though it had been promised, no real *base of stability* though this was one of the subdivisions of the discourse."[1]

In spite of all, the speech was very well received. Mirabeau wrote: "They were drunk with the desire to applaud, and they have applauded unto satiety." Indeed, this applause was the best proof of the prevailing optimism. It was literally true what a few months later Mirabeau wrote to his uncle: "There is not one commoner that did not come with very moderate sentiments to the National Assembly;"[2] nay, he was strictly within truth when, at a still later period, he asserted in one of his Notes for the court, that the "Assembly, in the first moments of its existence, was much less disposed to liberty than to slavery."[3] But while the optimism was very far from being coupled with radicalism, the levity, with which one held

---

[1] Œuvres, I. 171.
[2] Oct. 23, 1789. Loménie, V. 421.
[3] Oct. 6, 1790. Corresp., II. 218.

oneself excused by enthusiasm from all critical examination, proved that a thick film lay over the eyes, and this might easily prove a much greater danger, than a little less moderate views at the start would have been.

After the king and before Necker, the keeper of the seals Barentin had spoken. His speech, "mumbled out, in a very ungraceful manner," as Gouverneur Morris writes to his wife, was composed of some scraps of French history, bombastic panegyrics on the king and his government, and empty phrases on the necessity of hearty concert between the government and the people. But it contained one sentence of the greatest import. "The king has not changed the old form, each order meeting and deliberating by itself, and though it seems desirable to take the vote *per capita*, because that has the advantage of better ascertaining the general wish, the king wills that this new form be only adopted with the free consent of the States-General and with the sanction of His Majesty."[1]

Thus the only thing the government did was to set the orders by the ears. But however moderate the deputies of the third estate were, in this one question they could not yield, for to yield in this

Arch. Parl., VIII. 3.

was to abandon themselves and every possibility of reform. In this question, as Mirabeau declared on the 28th of May, "they cannot accept either judges or arbiters."[1] They could not fail to see this, so long as the government did not succeed in trebling the thickness of the film over their eyes. The government, however, from intellectual and moral imbecility, persisting in the mad resolution to let its way run between hammer and anvil, successfully punctured it. Barentin's announcement amounted to an admission in so many words, that the commoners were right. If there had been before any disposition among them to yield eventually, this explicit admission must have necessarily caused them to change their minds. But though the government acknowledged, that the commoners had reason on their side, it gave the case to the upper orders, not, however, completely and for good—only provisionally, and not even binding itself to the extent of definitely promising its consent, in case the orders should come to an agreement. To cap the climax, Necker declared that the king intended to speak "less as sovereign than as protector of the interests of the nation," and the privileged orders, which listened to the

[1] Œuvres, I. 210.

rest of his speech "in sullen or contemptuous silence," "very vividly applauded the homily on the deliberations by orders."

Mirabeau instantly warned him, with all the sternness and all the incisive solemnity of one who has a right and stands ready to take the judgment-seat, to beware of this applause. The very same day he wrote: " Let us hope that the minister of finance will at last understand that it is no longer time to trim; that one cannot resist the current of public opinion; that one must either be assisted or submerged by it; that the reign of intrigue, as that of charlatanism, is past; that the cabals will die at his feet if he be true to the principles, and that they will quickly unhorse him if he abandon them; that in the strength of an unheard-of popularity, he has nothing to fear but the desertion of his own cause; and that if, in the situation into which the kingdom is plunged, indefatigable patience is necessary, inflexible firmness is not less so."[1]

Whether the king could have dispensed with the States-General or not, it was as clear as the sun at noonday that, having convened them, the interest of the government itself as well as that of

[1] Œuvres, I. 177.

the country, imperatively demanded that they be enabled to go at once about the work they had been called to perform. Now nobody could tell when they would do so. With consummate skill Necker's policy of no-policy had plunged them into a bitter contest with each other and with the government sitting on the fence between them. This was not only not calculated to put an end to the "spontaneous anarchy," but whichever of the contending parties ultimately prevailed, a most portentous change of the whole situation would be the inevitable consequence of it. The first step towards a regeneration, requiring in the highest degree on all sides moderation, conciliation, and co-operation, was now a defeat with all its stings, which would keep on chafing and opening the wounds afresh. Besides, if the government was worsted—and it had to succumb or regeneration became impossible—it would be doubly difficult to regain the possibility of assuming the lead, in case its eyes should at last be opened to the fact that this was indispensable for its own safety as well as for the salvation of the country. It would be compelled to follow the victor—but whither? The commoners were most likely to push on in the heat of the contest much farther than they had ever intended to go; nay, it might easily become indispensable to do so in order to carry their point. They would then surely be most unwilling to retrace their steps, and it was at least very doubtful whether it would be at all within their power to do so. What Mirabeau said in his address of the 9th of July to the king held good even now: "There is contagion in passionate movements; we are but men; distrust of ourselves, the fear to appear weak, may push us beyond the mark; we shall be pressed by violent, extravagant counsels."[1] To persist in the order announced by Barentin was to force the commoners to put the government and the privileged orders to the alternative of surrendering at discretion, or having carried out to the letter the doctrine of Siéyès: the third estate is everything, and whoever is not of the third estate has no claim to being considered as of the nation.

All this, however, only rendered matters infinitely worse than they otherwise would have been; even without it there was every reason for most anxious solicitude. A high degree of short-sighted optimism was indeed required not to be aware of that.

The speech of the king, I said, was the virtual

[1] Œuvres, I. 314.

abdication of the government. But in whose favor? Let us look a little closer at the States-General.

Henry Morse Stephens says in his work on the French Revolution: "The deputies of the *tiers état* of the States-General, unlike those returned to the subsequent political assemblies, were simply men of local reputations and local ambitions. There had been no general conference for the selection of candidates and no electoral organization."[1] While the latter is correct, the first assertion is calculated to produce a very wrong impression. I, of course, do not intend to dispute that generally anything but uncommon perspicacity as to the future was manifested; but the instinctive feeling, that the country was entering upon a most momentous period of its history, was so universal and so vivid, that it would have been more than strange if, as a rule, those who offered themselves as candidates had been prompted only by local ambitions. They were surely in touch with public sentiment, and public sentiment as certainly was not confined to questions of local import. Nor is it true that, so far as France could boast at all of men of a different category, they were sim-

[1] Œuvres, I. 56.

ply men of local reputation. It is much more correct to characterize the States-General by saying that nearly every name, that from one reason or another was known to France before the revolution, is to be found in the representation of either the one or the other of the three orders.[1] Only a small minority, however, had any political experience of one kind or another, and literally not one had any parliamentary experience, for in this respect the provincial estates, of which some had been members, practically counted hardly for anything. Thus in the nature of the case, even the best lacked what was needed most. But grievous as the deficiencies in the mental outfit of the individuals must necessarily prove, they were comparatively of little moment. Looked upon as a whole, the sight was, in the fullest sense of the word, appalling. To realize the full import of the fact that the government had no programme, the other fact must be fully appreciated, that the

[1] La Marck writes: "En étudiant la révolution de 1789, il ne faut jamais perdre de vue que l'Assemblée nationale réunissait toutes les capacités, tous les talents, toute l'énergie, tout l'esprit, pour ainsi dire, du royaume, tandis qu'on ne rencontrait guère que de l'incapacité, de l'imprévoyance de la faiblesse, et certainement de l'insuffisance pour les circonstances dans les hommes qui composaient le ministère." —Corresp., I. 110.

States-General also had no programme, neither as a body nor as single orders. Yes, even the deputies of the third estate had none. Or rather these had only a negative programme, and, in a sense, that was even worse than none at all. "Everybody," writes Mirabeau in his 23d Note for the court, "knew what ought to be overthrown, nobody knew what ought to be erected."[1] I say, in a sense, this was even worse than no programme at all, for as to the theories imbibed from the writings of the philosophers, it was strictly true what Metra wrote: "It is an axiom that everything must be changed and broken down." Nobody knowing what to erect and the destruction of everything an axiom—what was that, if not starting upon a mad race to chaos? And where were the brakes that could have been applied to the wheels? The States-General not only had no programme, but they had also nothing else that could have exercised a restraining influence. A huge heap of particles swept together by the besom of chance, no previous tie of any kind whatever, no tradition, no corporate spirit, no party organization or even affiliation, mostly not even any personal acquaintance. Add to all this the national

[1] Sept. 7, 1790. Corresp., II. 163.

character, of which Mirabeau said: "It does not know where to stop, either in praise or in blame, either in its complaints or in its vengeance;"[1] and, "Who of us ignores that it is our blind and fickle levity[2] which has led us from century to century, and from blunders into blunders, to the crisis which afflicts us now and which ought at last to unseal our eyes, unless we are resolved to stay to the end of time children always mutinous and always slaves."[3]

During the contest and by the contest was brought into existence at least part of what the States-General were utterly lacking in the beginning and stood so badly in need of; but it was permeated by the strongest ferments, revealing every day more and more, that to a considerable extent the elements were as antagonistic as fire and water. To any parliamentary body this could have easily become fatal. What effect must it necessarily have upon this, which did not even know whether it was one or three, and the extent of whose authority was not circumscribed by any law, by any tradition, or by anything else! And this, in absolutely every respect, not only incon-

[1] Corresp., II, 212.   [2] *Mobile inconsidération.*
[3] Œuvres, I. 319.

gruous, but wholly nondescript body consisted of 1,200 members! Whether from so numerous a parliamentary body, even if possessed of all that this one lacked, sound legislative work could ever be expected, is, to say the least, very questionable. In times of universal, intense, and chronic excitement, it will always be in danger of degenerating into a mob. In case all I have mentioned is lacking, the only thing that can justly cause astonishment—even if every individual member be a sage—is, if it does not from the outset, uninterruptedly, and, in every respect, turn out to be nothing but a mob. The three speeches of the 5th of May had cast the die. From that moment it was a certainty that, if the vitality of the French people was proved by successful resistance of the commoners, their victory would lead to the condition so graphically described by Mirabeau in his 47th Note to the court: "I have considered as another obstacle the difficulty, or rather the absolute impossibility, systematically to direct an Assembly of such a vast mass, over which its most revered chiefs have only very little ascendency, and which eludes every influence. The direction of so numerous an Assembly, even if it had been possible at the moment of its formation, is no more so to-day, thanks to the habit it has acquired of acting like the people it represents, by movements always brusque, always passionate, always precipitate. It has its orators and its spectators, its theatre and its pit, its *foyer* and its stage setting; it favors talent when it is served by it; it humiliates it when it is crossed by it; no secret, no concert is possible in the midst of the clashing of self-love of which it is the arena; it deems itself too strong to try to enlighten itself, too far advanced to recede, too powerful to compromise." [1]

And this incongruous mass-meeting with nothing and nobody to guide it is not only an ordinary Legislature. It is also a Constituent Assembly. Surely, if there is a people on the face of the earth which ought to be capable of fully grasping what that implies, it is the people of this republic. Recall to your memory the history of your own Philadelphia Convention. A mere handful of men, all weighed and found not wanting in times that tried men's souls, all looked up to and revered as the wisest and best, all trained in every respect to an uncommon degree in the school of experience, only political and not social problems also their task—and even the political confined to a limited

[1] Corresp., II. 420.

field—and yet it is conceded by every single student of this period I have ever heard of, that they would surely have failed, if they had not started with the wise resolution to deliberate behind closed doors, and not to let the people know what they were doing until they had finished the arduous work entrusted to them. And now look at this picture: 1,200 men, untried, inexperienced, ushered into their official existence with a protracted and most bitter contest, not prompted by the same impulses, not striving after the same aim and end, discussing and framing the political constitution and the social structure of the country in the open market, and soon under the direct fire of the galleries.

This too was a legitimate consequence of the wrangle between the orders so dexterously initiated by Necker, and to realize what it meant, one only need remember what the *ancien régime* had made of the masses. To hold their ground against the alliance of the privileged orders and the government, the commoners were not over-scrupulous in examining the support offered to them by public opinion, and the voice of the masses also constituted a part of public opinion. Like the government, however, they too soon experienced that, as

Mirabeau had warned Necker, the only choice was between being assisted or submerged by it, and to make sure of its assistance, it soon became necessary to be always a step or two ahead of it. In consequence, leadership gradually changed into running in front in order not to be overrun. To facilitate the labors of the discordant mass-meeting of 1,200 [1] members, a self-appointed and ever fluctuating advisory committee, counting by thousands, joined them whenever it saw fit. The overwhelming majority of the Assembly was far from relishing this, but, as Mirabeau said, it was "forced" at the same time "to consult and to combat the multitude." [2] The consulting more and more prevailed over the combating, so that, according to the same authority, "the laws are more the work of the people than of its representatives." [3] When his ashes rested in the Pantheon, the fearful times came when, on the part of the successors of the Constituent Assembly, this consulting often became a meek receiving of orders. But he, too, lived through more than one dark day, on which things looked desperately like having come to that pass already. When the great debate on the veto-power of the king was going

[1] To be exact: 1118.   [2] Corresp., II. 163.   [3] Ib., l. c.

on, Camille Desmoulins wrote in the *Lanterne:* " Happily the incorruptible galleries are there, which always stand on the side of the patriots. They represent the tribunes, who assisted the discussions of the Senate on a bench and had the veto-right. They represent the capital, and fortunately the constitution is framed under the batteries of the capital."

The worst was that, as Mirabeau pointed out in the Note I have just quoted twice, the discordant and unguided mass-meeting was compelled to be at the same time an ordinary legislature and a constituent assembly. While it framed the fundamental law, it had to provide for the exigencies of the day, which embraced the whole life of the nation in every one of its aspects and relations, and which were of such urgency, that frequently a delay of a week or two could become fatal. No miracle could have prevented this from exerting a tremendous and most pernicious influence. It was a plain but most portentous truth which Mirabeau proclaimed on the 18th of September, 1789: The best constitution and the wisest laws are useless, if we do not know how to provide for the needs of the moment.[1] The course of events did not stop

[1] Œuvres, II. 158.

to allow the Assembly time in serene tranquillity to frame its laws and much less the constitution, but went on with terrific momentum. The actual conditions change from week to week, in a measure never before or afterwards experienced by any other people. And in this constant changing of conditions one fact swells from week to week into more disastrous prominence: the government virtually abdicates more and more also as executive, and the discordant and unguided mass-meeting, which has to be legislature and constituent assembly, gradually drifts into assuming also the functions of the administration.

Who that is able to discern these leading traits among the mad whirl of events, can be surprised that Mirabeau had to write: "One has undertaken to make a constitution in the midst of the tempests of public opinion, and the resistance of the two first orders having constrained the third to seek its force in the influence of the people, it was then compelled to satisfy it, to flatter it, to corrupt it, to associate it with all the parts of the administration, to refer everything to it, to do everything by it, to create all, to destroy all for it. Thus a constitution, which ought to have been an immortal work, is only a compound of measures dictated either by fear or hatred, by the most transitory circumstances, and by the needs of every moment.[1] Who can be surprised that the legislation did not even come up to the constitution, and that the actual condition was infinitely worse than either the constitution or the laws, the commonwealth steadily and at an increasing rate of speed gliding down towards the gulf of anarchy? There is one thing, not only surprising, but really astounding, and that is, that everything did not go infinitely faster and more completely to wreck and ruin, and that there was so much in the laws and in the constitution, that was a glorious and lasting achievement, not only for France but for Europe.

Aye, the States-General were a rudderless craft in a storm-tossed sea, carried by the currents straight on to the breakers, and the crew not only most grievously blundered, but also the deep stain of guilt spotted its garments profusely. But that this crew, thus collected, could, under such circumstances, make such a sail, bears a testimony to the genius and the high-soaring idealism of the great nation, than which there is none more glorious in its whole history.

[1] Corresp., II. 226.

www.ingramcontent.com/pod-product-compliance
Lightning Source LLC
Chambersburg PA
CBHW031349230426
43670CB00006B/482